Messages to Meetings

Brian Drayton

Inner Light Books
San Francisco, California
2021

Messages to Meetings

© 2021 Brian Drayton
All rights reserved

Except for brief quotations, no part of this publication may be reproduced, stored in a retrieval system, or transmitted in any form or by any means, electronic, mechanical, photocopying, recording, or otherwise, without prior written permission.

Editor: Charles Martin
Copy editor: Kathy McKay
Layout and design: Matt Kelsey

Published by Inner Light Books
San Francisco, California
www.innerlightbooks.com
editor@innerlightbooks.com

Library of Congress Control Number: 2021936998

ISBN 978-1-7370112-0-0 (hardcover)
ISBN 978–1-7370112-1-7 (paperback)
ISBN 978–1-7370112-2-4 (eBook)

New Testament quotations are translations by the author unless indicated otherwise.

Quotations from the Hebrew Scriptures are from the King James Version (KJV) unless otherwise noted. Rights in the Authorized (King James) Version in the United Kingdom are vested in the Crown. Reproduced by permission of the Crown's patentee, Cambridge University Press.

Three of the letters in this book ("Climate change a spiritual challenge," "Becoming again a witnessing body," and "Unity, disunity, diversity") were originally published by Beacon Hill Friends House, an independent Quaker nonprofit organization, residential community, and learning center in downtown Boston, Massachusetts, which also serves as the home of Beacon Hill Friends Meeting of the Religious Society of Friends (Quaker). Information on past and upcoming Friends House programs can be found on its website, www.bhfh.org. Reprinted by permission.

The author is grateful to Charles Martin and Erik Cleven for their encouragement of this project.

Contents

An introductory letter.. 1

1. To Friends in New England 3
2. For Multnomah Friends: On praying towards unity ... 5
3. Awesome: Psalm 111 and true worship—For ministering Friends gathered in Cambridge 9
4. As we reflect on our meetings' spiritual condition: A letter to my Friends.. 14
5. Climate change a spiritual challenge: A letter to New England Friends, in love to your souls, from a grateful child of earth 20
6. Becoming again a witnessing body: A letter to New England Friends...28
7. To ministers and elders gathering in West Brattleboro 33
8. To Friends, not to reason and judge too much about gifts, but to listen to the Witness, and not to fear 35
9. To Fresh Pond Meeting 39
10. To those who may be drawn in love to travel among Friends 43
11. The fear of the Lord is our treasure 45
12. Nurturing the Seed: To Friends in and around Berkeley...48
13. Not to be discouraged by the great challenges before us: To New England Friends 52
14. Friends, welcome prophets among us in these dark times! To New England's Meetings 55
15. It doesn't have to be this way: Proclaiming gospel values, with a note on "original sin" 58

16. To ministering Friends gathered in Northwest Quarterly Meeting 63

17. To Friendship Meeting 65

18. For ministering Friends gathering in Plainfield 68

19. Building our house in the storm: A letter to New England Friends 70

20. "That of God in every one": Can we not say a little more? 74

21. Unity, disunity, diversity or Some mysteries of the Holy Spirit's LIFE at work in its body's members hinted at: A letter to New England Friends 79

Bibliography 106

Notes 109

An introductory letter

Dear Friends,

I wrote the items in this collection out of a sense of requirement in conjunction with service in gospel ministry. The seed for many of these letters was a strong sense of unfinished business—as Friends used to say, I was not free of a particular place I'd been. After yielding to such leadings a few times, I became aware that such letters represented a kind of ministry that I should be alert to.

Letters of this kind were long as much a part of Quaker ministry as journals or, indeed, the traveling ministry itself. Friends of the first generation, in the mid-1600s, were often led to write to meetings or other groups, and such letters were one source for the practice of composing meeting epistles. Such epistles in turn formed the core material of the first books of discipline (called "books of extracts"), especially the advices. Before such meeting epistles, the first guidance about discipline can be found in letters from the first Publishers of Truth, beginning with William Dewsbury and including George Fox's many letters of counsel and guidance.

It is also the case that letters between individuals were an essential ingredient in the encouragement and support of ministry, the response to persecution, and the offering of pastoral care—and plain old news. Such letters have been published as devotional works; collections by Isaac Penington, John Thorpe, and Sarah Grubb come to mind.

In letters to groups and to individuals, Friends were well aware of the precedents in Christian history (and in the classical world as well), starting with Paul. Letters, even formally composed ones, have a feeling of personality and immediacy that can speak to the heart and "reach the Witness" for encouragement, instruction, or warning.

In these letters, I often find myself quoting other Friends, and this is not just because I am a quoting sort of person. I am very aware of all these past Friends as part of our community and of their deep insights, often hard won, about how the Quaker path can look and how spiritual growth in individuals and meetings can be encouraged. It is strengthening to intentionally keep their writings as part of our spiritual conversations today.

A couple of the items in this collection are adapted from messages given in a meeting for worship. I do not make a habit of noting what I have said when I am moved to speak. Very occasionally, however, it seems in right order to revisit a message and cast it into a form that may be of use in very different contexts, checking quotations and scriptural references for accuracy and unfolding an idea that was hinted at too obscurely when the ministry was being delivered.

I have added some small amendments by way of clarification (as I hope) to some items in this collection and have made other minor edits. In addition, as suggested by the editor, I have added explanatory endnotes and references.

It is my hope that these letters will be of use for individual reflection or meeting conversations. They were written originally out of a motion of love and with the intent that they might help some readers on their path towards the more abundant life that Christ promises and makes possible.

In Christian love your friend,

Brian Drayton

1. To Friends in New England

This letter was written under a concern and circulated by hand and by email December 7, 2014.

Dear Friends,

God's work to liberate us begins long before we are aware of it, and sometimes we need someone else to acknowledge the Light that they see working in us before we can acknowledge and accept it ourselves. This is why it is a very great gift to greet the Seed in one another.

When Mary understood that the child she was bearing, Jesus, was to be a message from God, she went to visit her cousin Elizabeth for comfort and counsel. Though Mary did not know it, Elizabeth also was carrying a child of promise in her own womb. Each woman was participating in an act of creation and renewal in which a basic process of human life—the bearing of a child—was somehow to be the vessel of divine action on a world-shaking scale. How hard it must have been to dwell at the same time with the daily, hourly experience of incubation and with the promise of great consequences to come! But when Mary arrived, the child in Elizabeth's womb leapt for joy, recognizing the new life hidden in Mary's care (Luke 1:41). The greeting from secret life to secret life enabled Mary and Elizabeth to understand more clearly the promise they both were fulfilling, which had long been in preparation.

So, Friends, when we greet the Seed as we feel it present in one another, we can feel more clearly what is unfolding under God's hand for us and through us. It is the same Seed in all, the life of Christ at work. As we come to recognize it in its clarity, we can wait with it in patience until we find ourselves free from things we need to let go of or free to take up tasks or practices that we know are laid on us so that we can accept them and give them the truth of action.

When we practice greeting the Seed in each other, we are guided, taught, and formed, so that our inward eye is sharpened to see it. Longing to see that Seed alive and lively in others, we can become more and more able to welcome its growth up through the barriers, the overburden, and the clutter that is keeping it down. In looking to greet the Seed, we find the living source of community, of spiritual formation, and of gospel ministry.

Then there comes victory; it is not ours, yet we share it. There is power, which is not ours, yet being love it transforms us. Mercy, patience, and courage come for our comfort and our use. Joy comes from the Light and is the joy of the divine life that all can share and feed upon with thanksgiving.

In Christian love, your friend,

Brian Drayton

2. For Multnomah Friends: On praying towards unity

This letter was written April 18, 2015, after I traveled in the ministry in the Portland, Oregon, area.

Dear Friends,

Since we were with you a few days ago, I have found that, when I sit in the quiet, I am not free until I share one thing more with you. This is to encourage you in love to pray towards unity as you follow your concerns. Indeed, this prayer towards unity may itself be a concern to follow when no other path or leading is discernible. What do I mean?

1. Imaginative participation. Prayer takes many forms, and some of those forms are available even to someone who does not think they know how to pray. A wordless, steady regard, in a time when one is quiet in reverence, is a powerful way of working—or rather of allowing oneself to be worked upon. When we are truly centered, even for a short space of time, we are tender, that is, vulnerable and teachable. If then we bring into that place a longing or need that is on us, it can be a time of discovery and movement and imaginative participation in the concern we are holding and the community we love.

2. Heightened awareness. One of the results of this kind of contemplation is heightened awareness. In that receptive place where we are most able to hear (or see or feel) the truth, we are often given fresh understanding. We may perceive more details about the community life—or one's own participation in it—and see connections, or even questions, that were not apparent before. As ever in such times of quiet openness, as we feel safe or grounded, we may be given to see barriers that need to come down if growth is to occur, or new things that must be learned, or rifts that must be mended. A deep fruit of this kind of work is an increase in inward spaciousness and freedom, a peace that is the peace of the ripening or opening seed, and a gift of thankfulness. It is quiet, but it is also the workshop of turbulent, organic creativity as in the stillness and tenderness all the materials of ourselves, our works, and our world can be in fluid contact. Remember that Jesus said, *"My peace I give unto you—not as the world gives, give I unto you"* (John 14:27 KJV).

3. Praying towards unity. The Spirit by which we are guided, and which underlies all our separate concerns, longs for, persuades towards, our unity. A frequent attention to the community, and a waiting to feel where the unity stands (beneath all our diversity), is a gift to oneself and one's meeting. Gifts are not elicited by demand or strength but are things received from love. The kind of prayer I am advocating is one in which our selves, and all the parts and actions of our spiritual body, are held lovingly and are known at bottom to be deeply connected. As we make this kind of attention, or attentiveness, a steady thread of our practice, we can find our way, experimentally, into an understanding—and an ability—to see, and then to live, in unity in some measure. We may well lose sight of the unity, but once we have had the taste of it we know that it can be found and felt again.

This unity may be expressed in many ways and may well grow into a strong, shared vision for community life. The beauty of this is that such a growing understanding, rooted in prayer as well as

2. FOR MULTNOMAH FRIENDS

hard work and good thinking, may be a fresh way to understand and share gospel living—remembering that the good news is the power of God to work liberation. This can be a way to live into a demonstration of that. *Thou shalt love the Lord thy God with all thy heart, and with all thy soul, and with all thy strength, and with all thy mind* (Luke 10:27 KJV).

* * *

When Darcy and I came away from our time with you, we were refreshed and encouraged by you and by the sense that we had been faithfully led among you. The encouragement, curiously, was a longing to be more ready for any next opportunity for service. This is often the way, that acting from a right place, being faithful in one's measure, is nourishing and healing, makes one humble in growth, gives capacity for further work under the Spirit's guidance—and gives a sense of hope and excitement.

Many of you, however, spoke of the familiar problem of action that is dispersing and may be mixed so much with fear or urgency that each one's work, however good, feels like a private matter and not vitally connected with others' activities. Even thinking through the logical ways that "your concern is related to mine" does not satisfy the need for substantive connection.

The prayer that I am writing of is a path towards safety, of practicing so that our actions and concerns are not scattering but are in some measure gathered in the Spirit—and once we live up to our measure, more will be given. This way is founded on longing and desire, a sense of need, a love of justice and truth, a watchfulness, and a faithful response to what is shown us. So many great souls have shown us how this path can be a place of rest as well as renewal, and as we are unified in ourselves, we find ways to come together as one community whose actions in the world are various but come with power out of the work of discovery, and unification, in the Spirit.

In Christian love, your friend,

Brian Drayton

Friends, whatever ye are addicted to, the tempter will come in that thing; and when he can trouble you, then he gets advantage over you, and then you are gone. Stand still in that which is pure, after ye see yourselves; and then mercy comes in. After thou seest thy thoughts, and the temptations, do not think, but submit; and then power comes. Stand still in that which shows and discovers; and then doth strength immediately come. And stand still in the Light, and submit to it, and the other will be hushed and gone; and then content comes.
—George Fox, Epistle 10 (1652)

3. Awesome: Psalm 111 and true worship—For ministering Friends gathered in Cambridge

In recent years, some New England Friends have come to feel a concern to occasionally gather Friends called to ministry or to spiritual nurture for mutual encouragement. This letter was written January 28, 2017, after a visit to one such group.

The fear of the Lord is the beginning of wisdom, and they that live by it grow in understanding.
—*Psalm 111:10 NEV*

Dear Friends,

1. Sometimes it's good to stop and reach down to the fundamentals. The Hebrew word translated as "fear" (*yare'*) in verse 10 of Psalm 111 can just as well be translated as "awe" in contrast to "terror" (*pachad*). The first has more of a spiritual connotation, the other more of a physical one.

I have often thought that we don't, these days, think enough about the "soul." Of course, the nature or substance or definition of "soul" is a problem, but then so is "life" itself as an abstraction or proposition. Even if "soul" is taken to be a metaphor or a placeholder, however, it is sometimes useful to reflect on what makes for soul health. For such health is foundational to all our actions as spiritual beings—it affects the quality of our activity, our words, and our deeds.

At the very least, it may be permitted to say that the soul is that which is engaged by true worship. By "engaged," I mean to include convicted, enlightened, nudged, reproved, refreshed, and all the other events that may happen when worship is alive and truthful. By "true worship," I mean worship in which something happens that relates to inward growth, an encounter with an Other (other than our will) that begins or nurtures or demands a change, first in inward condition and then in outward behavior.

Jesus was preaching no dualistic doctrine when he said, *Don't fear those that can kill the body but not the soul; fear rather the one who can destroy both body and soul* (Matthew 10:28). The master who affirmed God's love for the creation is reiterating here what he said in other terms: Seek first the kingdom of God and its righteousness, and all the other good things that we need for life will be added thereto, as they are without seeking for the birds of the air and the grasses of the field. The child of God is most fully alive when their allegiance is established on that foundation.

For me, at least, the experience of awe is the starting place. While it is present, it clears away all other engagements and presentations of self. It is anything but empty, though it is a state in which the little mills of thought and emotion cease from their grinding for a bit. As in other centering experiences, thought and emotion can be readmitted into the inward sanctuary once it's been cleared. But with awe, the fear of the Lord, it is not that my little interior space is reordered; despite myself, I am given to feel and see beyond myself.

My earliest memory is one of awe; I was transported by the sight of barn swallows wheeling amongst sunbeams pouring through gaps in the roof of a ruinous barn. Freedom, refreshment, and delight.

2. The second half of verse 10 in Psalm 111 moves from the intensity of the experience of awe to its extension into the world. The New English Version of the Bible

3. AWESOME: PSALM 111

seems understated when it says that those who "live by it" grow in understanding. The Septuagint says, "Good understanding [comes to, belongs to] to everyone who *practices* it" (where "it" refers to the wisdom, perhaps insight, one gains from awe). The Hebrew, I think, says something similar: that "good understanding [belongs] to all who *practice*" (awe and its consequent wisdom).

Thus, the psalmist, like Jesus, teaches that awe gives rise to wisdom (insight, understanding) *as one lives it out in practice*. We are to seek first the kingdom, but we are known by our fruits of word and deed—this is no purely interior event, but the changed heart brings forth treasures which in their measure change the world.

3. So, here we come back to the importance of seeking "true worship," worship in truth. In such worship, the divine life is known to be at work, and in its tendering effect we have evidence, assurance, that we can grow up further into freedom, freedom in the spirit of Christ, whose law is love and whose power comes through liberation as we accept the truth of our condition and the promise that we can walk fully as children of the Light. As Isaac Penington writes:

> He that hath the least taste of faith, knows a measure of rest, finding the life working in him, and his soul daily led further and further into life by the working of the life, and the heavy yoke of his own laboring after life taken off from his shoulders. Now here is the truth, here is the life, here is the sabbath, here is the worship of the soul.[1]

I know for sure that at times I worship for myself and do not seek to get beyond that. I may strive for silence, even achieve an inward silence, but it can be no more than a repose that asks for nothing further, a quiet that is not at all expectant. In itself, this is not bad, and rest of this kind is as necessary to the soul as sleep is to the body. But I must not fool myself: this is no more than a precondition for worship, not the thing itself. How often I sit in meeting with no profit but repose, going from it basically unaltered and no further along in faithfulness than before—not seeking to feel beyond the "first birth" in which I am using my own skill and will! As James Nayler writes of the will-worship Friends testified against:

> The first man worships a God at a distance, but knows Him not, nor where He is . . . and here he has fellowship with men, or with those he calls brethren. . . . And thus in vain does he worship.[2]

True worship, in which I have not only come to rest but have opened longingly towards a power or motion beyond my own, is known by its fruits, a change towards a life more and more freed from bondage. Nayler also writes:

> Before any can rightly worship God, they must wait to know His Spirit, that leads to know Him and His worship, and the matter, and manner; for all who do the same thing only as to the outward performance, do not worship God, because they worship not in the Spirit and power of God Himself. . . . [T]he way to be well-pleasing to the Father, is to wait in the light, till you feel something of the Spirit of life, which is in Christ Jesus, moving in you, and then to that join, in its power to worship.[3]

Such worship can disturb one's comfort and awaken one to the threatening, risky engagement with the dynamics of struggle, compassion, and witness—the Lamb's War.[4]

4. As a minister, I must be honest about the condition of my worship life, and aware of when it is not true. For when I am not come to true worship, I have not come to the place of availability, receptive to guidance and open

3. AWESOME: PSALM 111

to those with whom I worship. Not worshiping in truth, I am not serviceable.

Awe, the fear of the Lord, enables me once again to seek the place which opens to openness. I have known it, and every time I come there again I must observe, mark, taste, and feel it so that when I wander again, I know what to look for, what my soul indeed is hungering for, dull and distracted though it be.

And so I find that, whether I am in that condition of worshiping in truth or wandering from it, it is good to join with the psalmist and confess my gratitude to God, who knows how I long for the living water, and as long as I do long for it, God points me over and over towards it and directs my feet to the paths of praise.

Brian Drayton

4. As we reflect on our meetings' spiritual condition: A letter to my Friends

Each New England monthly meeting is asked to make an annual report to the yearly meeting on their spiritual condition for the previous year. It is a practice that meetings frequently feel the need to refresh to keep it serviceable. This letter arose out of a 2014 visit to Vassalboro (Maine) Quarterly Meeting.

Dear Friends,

At this time of year, our meetings are thinking about our "State of Society" reports. In the past few weeks, I have found myself often drawn to reflect on this work and on the service it can be to us to see our meetings' condition and, in doing so, our own as well.

Our practices can too often feel like customs or routines to follow out of habit or to maintain order. Yet we can, with prayer and imagination, come to them in the Spirit in which they were adopted and find in them renewed openings. The first operation of the Light is to show us our condition, and there also ability comes to follow it. In turning to the Light, we find renewal for our journey as a people gathered.

What I have been led to consider is, What are the evidences of a meeting's health? Activity, busyness, is no more evidence of a community's health than it is a sign of personal health. On the other hand, persistent quiet is not necessarily a sign of tranquility. I am concerned to lift up two kinds of evidence: the climate of the meeting and the ministry to people of different conditions.

4. AS WE REFLECT

Meeting Climate

Is there a climate of engaged love? Acceptance and hospitality are of great value, but the kind of love that healthy meetings have is a practical one that reaches further. Such active love is eager to see a growth in each member of the meeting of the fruits of the Spirit and is intentional about spiritual nurture to encourage that growth.

Do Friends voice and act upon the assumption that "each member hath an office [i.e., a gift] and is serviceable"[1] for the life of the whole? Are the marginal or shy, the young, the tired held in the kind of loving attention that does not press but is on the lookout for opportunities to see and name how each can serve according to their capacity and measure?

Is the meeting teachable towards unity in the Spirit? In our day, we are deeply aware of the diversity of our communities. Indeed, we often challenge ourselves to be yet more diverse and to include more kinds of people, from more conditions, than we have in the past. Out of such diversity can come a growth of insight and a greater capacity to reach and be reached by the Witness of God in others of different backgrounds. Sometimes the diversity of beliefs, and the many differing paths by which we have been gathered into our meetings, feels like the paramount truth of our condition, and while we are grateful, we can also feel weakened as a community and fear we are reduced to an association of isolated reporters: "I wouldn't want to generalize about Quakers, but what *I* can say is . . ."

Yet our God is a God of unity, not confusion, and our communities are places where the divine presence should enable us to feel the truth of the unity that God wills for us; indeed, that is our basic condition. Truth and love, justice and forbearance, compassion and courage are all different names for the life of the One as it is expressed in and through us. Yet, it requires an act of intention to pray towards, long for, that unity as well as for the patience and courage to seek how to name it or enact it as we have found it.

In the end, Friends, the most important question about a meeting's climate is, What is the spiritual hunger you share? If it is companionship, that can be achieved in many ways. If it is visibility and activity, these, too, can be achieved by various means. If it is comfort and quiet, and the preservation of the community's history, these also are goals within reach.

But any of these can be accomplished without any real growth of experience with the Spirit as a living, disturbing, creating, healing, transforming power. Are there any in your meeting who cry with the psalmist, "*As the hart panteth after the water brooks, so panteth my soul after thee, O God*" (Psalm 42:1)?

In that hunger lie wrapped up all the other yearnings for peace, truth, equality, simplicity, and community—and indeed these many faces of love and power all are seen to be different effects of seeking and dwelling, in our measure, in the Presence that we seek and sometimes experience.

Ministry for and to different conditions

The ministry of the meeting, which includes the *words spoken* and the *silent ministry*, and the *words or deeds of service or prayer* with individuals or groups at other times, is rooted in a listening, loving focus on the actual people gathered and on the One in whom they are gathered.

As you consider the meeting's condition this year, Friends, listen for the conditions within the community in compassion and honesty. Three conditions that have

4. AS WE REFLECT

come particularly to mind in my exercise are these: the "young" members, of any age, who are new to Friends; the "established"; and the "well-grown in the truth." Each of these conditions has characteristics that may require particular kinds of service to help them forward, and it is good sometimes for a meeting to reflect on whether the ministry is offering what it can under God's guidance.

In the "young," that is, those new to Friends, there may be exploration, enthusiasm, receptivity, and a need and desire to learn the foundations of the Quaker path. They need guidance, but not only instruction. They have come to you in curiosity, perhaps, but under that is a restlessness or inquiry, and it is through the witness of your acts and life joined with words of explanation and welcome that they will be helped to see that among you they can find a living path. Inquirers need to feel our humility but also where we are touched with fire and the Holy Spirit.

In "established Friends," there is a growth of discipline and order, a maturing exploration of and use of gifts, and a habit of bearing responsibility for the life and support of the meeting. But in this period, there can be an engagement with contradictions and continued mysteries in the understanding of Quakerism. Faith and discoveries that were nourishing and inspiring in the first days among Friends may feel stale or insufficient for the demands now encountered. New resources and opportunities are needed if such active Friends are to rediscover their spiritual childhood—the place of wonder and gratitude, openness and receptivity. Fire and the Spirit!

Those well grown in the truth have a tested understanding of the value of the diverse paths people can follow as well as the dangers of a mere celebration of diversity. They have an understanding of the pitfalls and dangers of life in the Spirit, for individuals and meetings, and a sympathy for questioning and doubt. Their experience has brought a reliance on the workings of the Lord in many situations, and they have learned to wait and listen; they have seen (or others have seen in them) a growth in tenderness, courage, freedom, and discipline in love and truth. At this stage, though, there are fresh challenges that come from habits long established, the same problems and challenges returning over and over. They can read the indicators of the meeting's long-term good or ill health and stability, its growth and depth; caring deeply, they can yet feel taken for granted and that their own seeking and spiritual thirst is not seen.

Fire and the Spirit—the baptism is needed at every stage!

People in each of these stages of their spiritual life offer ministry rooted in the questions and findings of that condition, but each stage also has its temptations and problems. In each stage there are times of dryness, of misplaced complacency, of frustration, and of hope. *Everyone* needs to receive nurture and love, in meeting and out, if their gifts and strengths are to be confirmed and to grow. *All* need exhortation or inspiration, instruction, reassurance, consolation, gratitude, and challenge—accompaniment in the Spirit as individuals trying to walk in the Light.

In closing

Friends, as you consider the meeting's condition and the conditions of the members, seek out the resources that the Quaker path can offer for the seeker, the finder, the certain and the uncertain, the mystic and the nonmystic, the contemplatives and the ones bearing concerns for witness. All these are sitting among us, sharing our common life; and, indeed, each of us may

4. AS WE REFLECT

well stand in each of these conditions at some time in our life.

Under the guidance of the spirit of Christ, by whose light and life our body can be ordered to work as one organism, we can do our best to see how truth and life prosper among us and be prepared to help each other as way opens. If nothing else, we can hold each other in that Light where the heart's secrets are known, even if we do not know them, and where grace and power flows, ministering to the divine growth in each other as we receive ability from God.

In that Spirit, our "State of Society" report can rejoice with discernment, and challenge forthrightly with love, for welcoming and for building up, and accept our doubts and failings with patience and compassion so that everything serves the Life we call by so many names, whose work is healing, wisdom, and unity.

In Christian love, your friend,

Brian Drayton

5. Climate change a spiritual challenge: A letter to New England Friends, in love to your souls, from a grateful child of earth

> This letter was written August 2, 2011, and distributed by hand during New England's yearly meeting that year. It was later revised and published by Beacon Hill Friends House, along with the letter "On becoming again a witnessing people," with a helpful introduction by William Taber of Fresh Pond Meeting (Cambridge, Massachusetts).[1]

Dear Friends,

I give thanks to God for the ways in which Friends are awakening to concern for the earth and for the right use of resources even as we recognize that much remains to be done in response to the gathering force of climate change. We see and understand, too, that many other aspects of social justice and peace are linked now to the causes of, and possible responses to, climate change. We all can mourn or rage against these things, but why is it we cannot as a people make some clear witness? In sitting with this question, I have been led to write this letter to you with the hope that our spiritual witness and our environmental witness can be mutually strengthened and become more and more integrated. In the midst of this great and confusing crisis, we have an opportunity to fully engage in social action while also moving together towards more abundant life in the Spirit, which, if we find it, will be our greatest gift to our brothers and sisters in this world.

What is a 'spiritual challenge'? Most often, when someone names a 'spiritual challenge' they are identifying a difficulty or dilemma that confronts them

5. CLIMATE CHANGE

(or us). But what is the exercise that is demanded of us? I feel a need to speak more concretely. After all, if I say that walking the length of the Appalachian Trail constitutes a physical challenge for me, I can say precisely what it will require of *me*, in my current physical condition. It constitutes also other kinds of challenges: What do I do about my job? What will I need to carry with me? What problems will it pose for my family? and so on. These are questions whose answers come out of the material and situation of my life and almost always will be the names of tasks I must engage with if I want to respond to the challenge I have heard and accepted.

A spiritual challenge is one that requires us to grow because it is hard to integrate with our prior spiritual beliefs and habits. It demands some definite change in the way we act on and interpret the world and our condition, and it may require us to seek and use spiritual, intellectual, community, or physical resources to guide and feed the growth required. If we engage with such a challenge wholeheartedly, we will know we have met it, for the time being, by the reward of peace or a sense of inward reconciliation, by a sense of clarified under-standing, by a removal of some fear and sense of insufficiency, and by a renewed understanding of and faithfulness to our most essential spiritual commitments.

Why is climate change a spiritual challenge? There can be more than one answer to this! Here is my answer. As an ecologist, I track the science that is pouring in from every continent. Storms are growing bigger, weather more volatile, the Arctic has warmed perhaps 10 degrees in the past 100 years, species are moving or declining, droughts are becoming more intense, and the ocean is warming and becoming more acidic. Meanwhile, although many individuals are acting in response to the message of the data, political systems, which alone can effect the massive changes needed in the time available, are mostly ignoring the issue or at best are making token progress (as measured against the speed and size of the climatic changes happening). As a result, the world has entered a time that will be increasingly miserable, first in the poor areas, then across the globe. My grandchildren will see humans struggling in an impoverished world, with consequences unfolding for societies, economies, cultures, governments, and families.

To state this picture in other words, **the challenge is *desolation*.** There is grief and alarm at the loss of much that is beautiful and valuable in itself and at the consequent increase in suffering that will accrue to our ever more numerous human family. The changes we have set in motion will take decades to fully unfold, and it will be centuries before a new equilibrium is reached. At the time I am writing this, even if dramatic measures are taken in the next five years, we will only be able to somewhat soften the blows that are coming. The temptations to self-preservation at all costs, to competition and exclusiveness, will only rise because these are the most natural responses to crises that are already under way and indeed are accelerating. Moreover, our political systems by and large have developed in such a way that they are now best suited to serve a few powerful interests rather than the common good.

Beyond the invitation to anger and despair that the science news brings daily, I have therefore found myself losing illusions that, I realize, have been sources of hope but cannot any longer be relied upon. Some of my hope has been placed in *social structures*, such as government or other political agencies, which can enforce or implement large-scale social change of certain kinds. It

5. CLIMATE CHANGE

is increasingly likely that the major social structures will not respond in time to prevent protracted climate disruption. Some of my hope has been wedded to the idea of *progress and reform.* God's will is peace and justice, abundance, *agape,* and creation—but I no longer see how this translates to "progress" as Americans and optimists have usually meant it. Finally, I have placed stock in *knowing,* being able to comprehend not only my personal dilemmas but also the trends in which I am embedded. And I must admit that the hope that I have in knowing really reflects my deep desire to have control over my life for my own well-being and that of those I love.

We have not confronted the spiritual challenges of climate change until we recognize that some of our grounds for hopefulness are false and that we need again to ask where the Holy Spirit and the gospel story (including its later Quaker chapters, in some of which we are appearing right now) can be found in the midst of it all. At such a time, indeed, we are challenged to bring our grief and our need before the Living God. Many Friends have experienced surprising grace when driven to such an extremity, seeing that many of their props and resources were unreliable—"When all my hopes in them and in all men were gone, so that I had nothing outwardly to help me, nor could I tell what to do . . ."[2] We cannot tell God what to do, but we can know some things about how God moves among us.

When false hopes are removed, true hope can be discovered. It may be that our calling as a people is to be intentional about descending into the depths as we encounter them and then waiting there for the power to call out in thanksgiving and in a hope that lives without any illusion of control. If Friends as a people could testify first and foremost to the Spirit from which we learn love and the grace of a thankful heart, then indeed we can speak both power and love to our frightened, angry, disoriented time. The speaking will come with power as it comes from a life empowered by the work of the Holy Spirit in and through us, and as we open to true concerns, our work will bring consolation as love carries us past fear, even in calamitous times.

True concern. In the past few years, we New England Friends have sought hard to bring the resources of our yearly meeting to bear upon our sense of insufficient faithfulness. The frustration and confusion that have often resulted from this search suggest that we are not looking in the right places for the way forward and that we may not have gotten clear, each of us in our own hearts, about what the roots of our urge for action may be. We have not yet been drawn into the complex, empowering, and risky condition of concern—of seeing how a particular person, issue, place, or need is for us an essential and unavoidable next stage of our spiritual life. We may see that something is cause for alarm or regret or outrage, but it may remain an outward threat only until by the action of the Spirit some link of service and necessity is forged. Until that gap is closed, my activism will not reach to my core, nor will it be fed from the divine life. I may be under preparation, but I am not yet sent! A concern is, in a real sense, a spiritual challenge, and so it is particular, or makes particular demands, on each of us, even if we feel the concern to be widely shared. In fact, for each of us, the shared concern is really unique because it confronts each of us with the limits, uncertainties, and temptations that are ours alone; and, however supported by our Friends/friends, the inward response to the challenge must take the form of inward change in each individual.

True resources. Friends figured out long ago that if we are really to take seriously the realization that "Christ

5. CLIMATE CHANGE

has come to teach his people himself"[3] so that it is the foundation of our worship, our business practice, and our daily personal life, we must remain teachable and inwardly available. Early on, we discovered or were led into practices that could enable us to grow spiritually within our communities, whether under the challenges of our daily life or under more unusual ones (and these are not unrelated, since our faithfulness in small things prepares us for faithfulness in greater ones, including in outward action and witness). These practices are simple but not easy:

1. Watchfulness. Wait, wait, and wait again for understanding, for an opening path, and for the power to follow it. But we must beware because this can be done in a hardened, hasty, individualistic mindset. If we are to live with integrity the gospel life we are called to, our waiting must also probe this central question: *Can I feel how this leading, at its base, is one more outflowing of God's love? Can I see, at least dimly, how that love sharpens and corrects my view of the people and things I am called towards?* If we wait to feel where the current of love flows before we speak (in meeting or outside it) or act, the resulting integration of our actions with the Light will be rewarded in unexpected ways.

2. Prompt obedience. Friends from the beginning have recognized that the outward fruits of the inward life are cultivated by our accepting the Light we're given and acting on it in the smallest matters. We must be wary of the temptation to postpone action until something "really worth our effort" comes along. If we wait deeply enough, we will find that our anxiety about impact will be lifted from us because we can see that the fundamental message is the love of God as we can embody it, and this is at work in

many lives and many places. *To those who have, more shall be given* (Matthew 13:12).

3. Suffering or growth pangs. Taking the step that is given to us, and not outrunning our Guide, we will find that our inward process, now incarnated in our action, has outward consequences. These can include reactions (in ourselves or others) that are unpleasant and discouraging; "suffering" can take many forms visible and invisible, more or less understandable to others and tolerable or intolerable to oneself. These may range from self-doubt and questioning, to puzzlement or ridicule within our community, to inconvenience and complications in our outward affairs, to much more serious threats or pains. These sufferings may weigh on us and perplex us even if we are at the same time able to keep in touch with the joy that is rising as we move forward in a true leading.

We need to listen to questions, to recognize that it is possible we may be wrong, and to stay teachable, but the consequences of our earnest and loving attempts to be faithful will be both lesson and reward. Our friends can help us sort through it all, and that may be part of the nourishment that comes, but each of us bears our own cuts and bruises, and the healing in the end comes from within.

4. Proclamation and thanksgiving. What a gift it is when someone tells us how their concern arose, how they learned about it and prepared for it, what it took to feel how it was love at work, what journey they were taken on (however humble)! We need that witness more than any other because it kindles the life in us and gives us the hope that comes from truth enacted. We need to help each other give thanks for any step forward upon this way. We need to help each other practice telling the story—the whole story,

from inside out and outside in. If you act on a true concern, in love, you have changed the world in at least two ways: you have done your task, but you have also had to be changed to be best able to do it—just as Penn wrote about the first Publishers of Truth: "They were changed men themselves, before they went about to change others."[4] And, it is also important that we encourage and nurture gifts of proclamation and teaching, a servant ministry that invites and urges to more abundant life, that reflects the life at work in us all, and that helps us do the work each of us is called to, which is unique and precious.

Oh, Friends, remember, it's a miracle that we see unfolding when any of us feels a true concern, however small the motion! This is God at work, the waters of life flowing, the Seed stirring and strengthening as we give it hospitality. It is to us and through us, for our friends and in some measure for the sweet, inexhaustible Life that seeks to flow through all and has its witness everywhere in the earth and in every heart. Can we see it? Do we long for it? It comes often as just a morsel, but receiving it and feeling the gift and the communion of it, we will be fed and will have more than enough to share and share in turn till no one can say who started the feast, but each gives thanks to the Fountain of Miracles, for the birds, the air, the green leaf, and the spiritual bread sufficient for the day. Our vocation is towards joy and fullness of life—Oh! Taste and see that the Lord is good!

Brian Drayton

6. Becoming again a witnessing body: A letter to New England Friends

> I wrote this letter in 2011, and it was circulated that year as Friends were laboring to know and articulate a unifying witness. This and the preceding letter were later published in pamphlet form.[1]

Dear Friends,

Let us not speak falsely of our condition as a people. Jeremiah said, *"The false prophets dismissively 'healed' the shattering of my people, saying 'Peace, peace,' but where is there peace?"* (Jeremiah 6:14, my translation). We Friends in New England often act and speak as members of an association or interest group, not as members of one body unified by a common life or as a people gathered by the workings of a precious and holy Spirit. But we also speak and worship together, yearning for unity, for peace amidst our works and concerns, and for adequacy in the face of our lives and our times.

Friends, let us continually help each other remember that unity is not an accomplishment or a product but a process, a living process that requires the food and care appropriate to itself. A living body maintains its health in the face of abrasive, down-tearing, consuming forces by constant upbuilding, nourishment, rest, and creative action. The result is a sense of well-being, of flourishing, which speaks of a body and mind in balance. When we live as members of one spiritual body and that body is flourishing, we and our body will give evidence: patience, love, mutual forbearance, eagerness for good works, courage in the face of doubt or trouble, compassion, simplicity, truthfulness, teachableness, joy. If someone should examine our condition and find these alive in us,

6. BECOMING AGAIN A WITNESSING BODY

find them reliably to be true of us, then we can hope with some confidence that our flourishing has roots in the life of God flowing through us, which John's gospel called *Logos*, which is God's creating and healing power.

This in truth is the gospel, the power of God that works for our liberation, for each of us, but that also makes us know how and where we are one and where we can be confident of that unity. Jesus' last commandment was that his friends love each other as he had loved them, but at the last supper (John 17:21), he prayed that they all might be one, as Jesus and the Father were one; and through Christ they might be one with them. Where daily waiting in silence and expectancy comes to be characteristic of us as a people, we participate in the process of challenge and transformation that prepares us for the unity Jesus prayed for and equips us for. If our worship does not work a change so that we bear the fruits of the Spirit and the marks of those who have met with a living power beyond and yet within them, then our worship is *not yet true enough.*

Worshiping in truth day by day, we can avoid mistaking the benefits of this powerful common living for its essence. From that unity we can speak with power, act with endurance, awaken the sleepers, and invite others to the great work of living justly, creatively, and without fear, in balance with the natural forces upon which our bodies and our cultures depend. But we cannot manufacture that power, that truth, that fearlessness if we are not living in unity. Now, therefore, in a time when our unity feels fragile, let us practice unity by seeking each other's well-being and faithfulness.

In recent years, New England Friends have grown more accustomed, as a people, to acknowledge that there are diverse gifts among us, but we have not yet gone far enough in this work. We are called further—to act on, act in, the expectation that all can be faithful stewards for the gifts' sake and for each other's. As we are diligent in our own faithfulness and worship more and more in truth, we will grow ever more aware of how our own callings are bound up with the common life, and we will find more ways not only to assert that connection but also to affirm and forward it in concrete and specific ways. Let us receive concerns with joy, as the evidence of God's action each in our time, day, and measure, and be eager in praying for and nurturing these gifts, loving our neighbor's concern as if it were our own. But we need to work to live up to the truth long taught in all spiritual traditions that prayer is not just an interior event. For it to be a truthful transaction with the Divine, it must ultimately shape action. So, let us challenge ourselves and each other often, asking, *What concrete things have I done* to show my welcome for another's gifts so that I rejoice to feel the growth of God's life in them and feel myself nourished thereby?

Friends, remember how Isaiah rebuked the people of his time:

> *[T]his is a rebellious people, lying children, children that will not hear the law of the LORD: Which say to the seers, See not; and to the prophets, Prophesy not unto us right things, speak unto us smooth things, prophesy deceits: Get you out of the way, turn aside out of the path, cause the Holy One of Israel to cease from before us.* (Isaiah 30:9–11).

Isaiah was sent to a people who had grown unfaithful to spiritual and ethical teachings. The conventional prophets were committed to giving the people what they asked for—complacency and comfort—rather than speaking the truth for their troubled times and pointing the path to life in harmony with God and ultimately with each other.

6. BECOMING AGAIN A WITNESSING BODY

But what would have happened if the people, yearning for spiritual health, had confronted these teachers prophetically, saying, "We are grateful for the motions of God in your life. Help us better know and live in the life of the Holy One. Tell us the truth in which we can be free. David once sang, *Some trust in chariots, and some in horses: but we will call upon the name of the Lord our God* (Psalm 20:7), seeking to learn from God the path of life. We want this to be true of us! Be faithful in your work so we can be faithful in ours. Be faithful in your life so we can be faithful in ours!

What will happen if we can learn to listen prophetically in this way to the motions of divine life in each other, expecting and calling each other to occupy and live fully in our several gifts, knowing that we need each other's faithfulness like a tree needs the sunlight and the rain?

Paul writes, *The eye can't say to the hand, "I don't need you," nor can the head say to the foot, "I have no need of you"* (1 Corinthians 12). Feel into this: We *need* each other, as a body needs all its parts. And Christ, the head, needs our feet and hands and eyes—and these need the head and the life that circulates and nourishes all parts in one enlivening stream. It is from this mutual need and experience of the common life that a witnessing body is fed and grows in strength, not by declaration or by assertion of unity; these articulate hope or announce our condition but cannot create or substitute for the shared living, the actual spiritual organism.

The gospel life is one, as God is one, and so all God's people, as they are in that life, are one. Sometimes we must take that on faith, when the unity is hard to see or feel. We can make a precious testimony if we daily seek to feel where that unity lies but also to enact it as part of our discipline as servants of that life. In this, Jesus promised we would find joy, as we can sometimes declare, out of our own experience.

In Christian love, your friend,

Brian Drayton

7. To ministers and elders gathering in West Brattleboro

I wrote this letter in September 2018 to an informal gathering in West Brattleboro, Vermont, of concerned Friends from across New England.

Dear Friends,

It is a great encouragement to know that you are gathering today. Since I cannot join you, I make so bold as to visit by letter. When there is so much work to do, and there seems to be so few doing it, a meeting like this is a precious time, and I think we cannot neglect meeting each other, writing to each other, praying for each other, remembering each other. It is urgent for us to find these ways of connection with our yokefellows and to take delight in the work done in us at these times.

Samuel Bownas famously wrote that the ministry is a birth,[1] and so I have learned in my degree. Those who accept the calling to service in ministry or eldership undertake a new journey of growth and spiritual exercise. Daily there is a supply of nourishment from the Lord, often in ways unexpected beforehand: new understandings about dwelling in humility, fresh opportunities to learn patience and watchfulness, new insights about the nature and constraints of divine love. When there is a chance to gather with others who accept and share the same work (each in their own fashion), there are so many things to share, learn, mourn, and give thanks for!

So, your meeting can have no outcome more important and sweet than deep and tendering worship together in which you can discover beyond words the unity you share with each other and with all your brothers and sisters who share the same calling to serve in love the spiritual life of those to whom they are sent. Rooted into that place of peace and safety, you are freed to tell and hear each other's stories, allowing yourselves to be pruned, watered, and further prepared to speak, act, pray, and wait in the awareness of the love at the heart of all. From that awareness, your work, our work, contributes in its measure to the reconciling work of Christ.

The reward is joy. Alleluiah!

In Christian love, your friend,

Brian Drayton

8. To Friends, not to reason and judge too much about gifts, but to listen to the Witness, and not to fear

> I wrote this letter to New England Friends in 2019 and published it on my blog, *Amor Vincat*.[1] It arose from a concern to encourage the work of naming and cultivating gifts in our meetings, which often brings meetings into hard exercise.

Dear Friends,

We are weakened, and the Seed suffers, because we are so reluctant to welcome and encourage spiritual gifts that are emerging among us. Life is rising fresh in young and old, and we say we want to encourage it but we talk and judge it down. So, we are lukewarm, and our growth is stunted. If gifts are not welcomed, they cannot be nurtured. If they are not nurtured, they will not be exercised. If there is no exercise, there can be little learning by individual or by meetings. So, we are always starting over, and we gain no wisdom.

Our meetings' descriptions of our spiritual condition each year speak clearly of our longing for nourishment, for learning, for power to live in the way the Spirit of Christ (however named) calls and leads us. Yet, when gifts start to move in someone and Friends take notice, our caution is so great as to wound and discourage the little, tender openings. Those who are timid and need cultivation in the work are often not even noticed, and we teach each other timidity and fear even though Paul urged us to desire earnestly the best gifts for the community of the Spirit to thrive.

How many teachers we need! How many counselors and comforters, experienced in prayer and the care of souls! How many writers, how many inspired, gifted stewards of our means and business! How many messengers from the witnessing Spirit speaking to that in others! How many witnesses in love for naming the power of evil, in our own beloved society and beyond, and for the healing of its wounds! How many peacemakers and mourners, watchers in prayer, and gifted rejoicers! All these should be well grown in the truth, which takes time and practice and incubation by loving insight.

We are full of fear, Friends, fear of each other and of the power of God. We are afraid to say that that one has a gift that others do not—because we do not trust that each has a gift and is serviceable. We do not feel how each part of the mystical body is needed in its difference and has holy value if exercised as the Light and Wisdom guides it to. Jesus asked, *"If salt loses its savor, how can it be made salty again?"* (Matthew 5:13). In the same way, the eye cannot say to the hand, I have no need of you, but if the hand never reaches to work, to point, or to caress (while the eye looks out and does its part), then it does not serve but only stays a dead weight.

When a gift arises in someone who wants to be faithful, they feel fear—that they are mistaken, that they have nothing to offer, that they will do wrong. It is for us to seek to the Witness in ourselves and feel what answers, and we must seek in honesty. Is there life coming there? We know that the Spirit pours out gifts for our needs in each community. What else should we do but be on the lookout for them and welcome them in their first appearance?

The Witness yearns for abundant life and can give power to live it. How is this power seen? It is seen when love is felt, when hindrances made up of fear or habit or

8. TO FRIENDS, NOT TO REASON AND JUDGE

wounds are weakened or taken away. With the ability to see one's chains comes guidance towards freedom, and with each step that way comes a taste of joy and courage. The Witness leads peacewards; it is the root of every spiritual gift and occasion to enact it. If Love is witnessed in our Friend or in ourselves, then there is life in the gift and the gift is for us all so the life coming through it will be for all. Make sure, make sure, that the first word said to a gift-birth is "Love"! Then, guidance, practice, form, and balance can be developed, and methods and techniques can have their place. The experienced travelers who have walked that path and know that kind of service and its costs should come forward to share the stories of their journey in the work, offering gifts of joy as well as warning. Growth and learning come in the forming and doing of service—this we know experimentally!

If we listen to the love in the voice of the Witness, fear is taken off and reasoning and judgment can become tools seasoned with wisdom. Remember, remember, that the greatest in the kingdom of heaven is the servant of all. We say to the world (often with self-congratulation) that "we are all ministers," but we are fearful of making that truly happen, of dedicating the time, patience, and effort to help each other know what our service is and how to build it up, how to cultivate our talents like good craftspeople through apprenticeship to mastery, each of us working to assemble and sharpen our tools and our fitness for the work, making our true service our delight and daily concern.

Friends, there is no time but this present, and our meetings and our world, in their weakness and turmoil, require generosity of spirit, not penny-pinching. So much the more, if we wish to be a prophetic people and a school of prophets, must we cling to love and let it season our judgment and draw us to make real the dear fellowship of the common life of the Spirit, which the first Friends knew as Christ come again in the bodies of his friends, as Immanuel who appeared and appears as a little, helpless thing unadorned and unlooked for but promising much.

In Christian love, your friend,

Brian Drayton

9. To Fresh Pond Meeting

Darcy Drayton and I were active in the founding of Fresh Pond Meeting (Cambridge, Massachusetts) in the late 1980s, and we have maintained strong ties of affection to the meeting since we moved north in 1996. We were able to be present as the meeting considered how best to encourage the ministry of a particular Friend, and this February 2004 letter was written in response to that gathering.

To Friends in Fresh Pond:

It was good to visit Fresh Pond Meeting this past Sunday and to sit in worship and conversation with you. In the quiet today, the following thoughts arose that I felt I should share in love.

I should say at the outset that I am not writing to advocate any particular course of action with regard to business now before you. I am moved by a sense I had of the condition of the meeting and by my engagement in concern and interest for the meeting's life.

Even though you have specific cases before you concerning whether and how to support a particular Friend, I urge you to consider that the larger challenge is to understand how the emergence and faithful use of gifts relates to the health and life of the meeting and even to its nature as a spiritual community. From this understanding will come fresh ability to explore how to nurture these gifts. I should say from the outset here that Friends traditionally have seen concerns and leadings as gifts as much as the personal capabilities, etc., that we usually think of when we speak of "gifts."

Although gifts come through individuals, Friends have seen them as given in the community and in some sense for the community. The image we have used is of the community as the body of Christ. In that vision, the different gifts and works that appear are essential to the health of the whole. Therefore, while Friend X may have a calling to work with the homeless, or to combat slavery, or to some other work outside the meeting, this gift is also to and for the meeting if it is acted on faithfully. This is because the faithful use of the gift will reveal more about the love and guidance of God at work among us, the transformations and learnings we must undergo in responding to that love and guidance, and the reliability of the Spirit as the bond of unity and the root of compassion and peace that is beyond human contrivance. We are pathfinders together.

It is for this reason that a gift or leading should entail communications from the Friend under concern to the meeting and to others who have the same (or a similar) concern. The ways that God leads us, the difficulties and the blessings that we encounter, and the ways that we learn from our mistakes as well as our successes—all of these are vital nutrients for the community as it seeks to understand better and better how to realize the meaning of the gospel in the present time. It is in this way that we put our faith to the test: is it real or make-believe?

Yet, the benefits of a gift do not accrue if the fit is not used. The Friend who has the gift will not grow in the spiritual life if they do not act on it to the best of their ability, in all humility and with an eagerness both to do and to learn in the doing. Furthermore, the gift is not well used if the Friend does not act on it in a way that tests, refreshes, and deepens their life in the Spirit with growth in sweetness, humility, and courage. While the ultimate responsibility for this lies with the individual, the meeting can make a significant difference, perhaps play a decisive role, in enabling the Friend's faithfulness.

9. TO FRESH POND MEETING

The forms that this work takes you are well aware of—discernment about the nature of the calling, guidance about timing and about the requisite preparation, support and feedback in times of doubt, support when it's time to lay down the work, restraint in times of confusion or overconfidence, insistence on communication, and, most important, receiving with joy the evidence of divine life in the concerned Friend. There is a faithfulness in acknowledging a gift with thankfulness that is as important as the faithfulness in acting upon it. Thankfulness will permeate the guidance and discernment that the community gives, and this will comfort and refresh the concerned Friend. Thankfulness sweetens all.

The life of watchful dependence upon the Spirit of Christ day by day is a hard road, sometimes because it feels difficult or painful but sometimes just because it requires a real maturation, a growth in "mastery," where the mastery comes in learning to listen, to act, or to wait as the Lord requires. It takes time, and as with any craft we learn much from our colleagues and friends. The lessons along the way become a real source of joy because even when we encounter failure or reproof, this contributes to our better understanding, our patience and humility, and our reliance upon and openness to the divine love that keeps expressing itself in our lives in a myriad of ways.

Dear Friends, I felt among you a lot of life, a lot of concern, a lot of faithfulness. Yet, I also felt a sense of hunger for deeper life and some coolness or hesitancy about letting the Spirit take over "too much." Caution is not fatal to the life of the Spirit, if the caution is flavored with a desire for faithfulness. By contrast, fear does kill or stunt the growth of God's good plant in us, just as frost can kill a tree's branches, fruit, or too-shallow roots. We can get caught in a cycle of wanting, talking, thinking, and imagining but not enacting our walk with God, pacing in circles and feeling the weight and discouragement of missed opportunity. . . . So, I hope that you will seek to understand what fears are at work and bring them to God in all honesty. I cannot imagine what paths will then open up, but the ones that do will be bathed in light.

In Christian love, your friend,

Brian Drayton

Now to the soul that hath felt breathings towards the Lord formerly. . . I have this to say: Where art thou? Art thou in thy soul's rest? . . . Is thy laboring for life in a good degree at an end? And dost thou feel the life and power flowing in upon thee from the free fountain? Is the load really taken from off thy back? Dost thou find the captivity redeemed and set free from the power of sin . . . and he which led thee captive from the life and from the eternal power, now led captive by the life, and by the redeeming power, which is eternal? Has thou found this, or hast thou missed of it? Let thine heart answer. Ah! Do not imagine and talk away the rest and salvation of thy soul. . . art thou here in the living power, in the divine life, joined to the spring of life, drawing water of life out of the well of life with joy? Or art thou dry, dead, barren sapless, or at best but unsatisfiedly mourning after what thou wantest?

—Isaac Penington, 1661[1]

10. To those who may be drawn in love to travel among Friends

> This letter arose in February 2016 after a gathering of ministering Friends in which some expressed discouragement.

Dear Friends,

In the Light, I am very grateful for your faithfulness, however small you feel it to be; it is precious. If you are faithful in your measure, much work is done to encourage others, to respond to the motions of the Spirit in their lives. I wish I could talk with each of you; you know how important it is for us to meet our Friends sometimes face to face. Since I cannot, I make so bold as to send this letter. I am led to lift up some of the effects of such visits in the hope that something in these reflections may help, encourage, or strengthen you if you travel in the future.

>1. A visiting Friend, come to worship with us, shows us that God's love is at work and has moved in this Friend to bring them here. We need this evidence! When we are cold, distracted, and inwardly dry, a visit may open a path to refreshment. When we are feeling spiritually well and alive, a visit encourages us in the sense of God's abundance and in our own desires to follow the Guide more closely. I encourage you, if you can do it from that pure love, to let Friends know that you were led to them that day—said without self-importance but as a matter of fact, this makes explicit and substantive the simple gift of presence.

>2. Your visit makes visible the flow of life throughout the spiritual body, from the divine root

through the smallest reaching twigs of the vine. The life circulates in many ways visible and invisible, but "living epistles" are irreplaceable gifts of personality, and when you, the visitor, return home, you bear those Friends and their place away with you and leave something of yourself among them. Bound in worship, sealed by presence with all its dimensions, both visitor and visited are enlarged. It may be that your prayer and theirs is enriched, fed by the recollection of the encounter, and your mutual accompaniment is renewed as you sit in the quiet.

3. If you make a visit with the awareness that love is at least part of your reason, you are opening yourself to growth and spiritual formation. Listening is at the base of faithfulness; coming in love, you will find something to nourish and challenge you in the voices, customs, concerns, and flavor of the meeting you are visiting. Loving interest opens our hearts, eyes, minds; seeking to be faithful, we learn where we are strong and where we are not. We learn to depend on more than knowledge, custom, or appearances for the Spirit is more lively and radical than these in its smallest movings. We teach the most important lesson by being teachable ourselves.

Friends, when we visit each other, we can come to know each other better on many levels. Each kind of knowledge can strengthen the fabric of our community so that we can better perceive and receive the Light and follow its leadings in our measures. As you go and as you come home again, seek to feel the divine love present and *to name it*. In the power of that love, nourished by shared worship, work, conversation, or play, we all will be more able to pray towards unity. *This is my commandment: Love one another as I have loved you* (John 13:34).

In Christian love, I am your friend, Brian Drayton

11. The fear of the Lord is our treasure

This is the substance of a message I gave in a meeting for worship on May 29, 2017.

Many of us are feeling fatigued and burdened by the condition of the society we live in. On top of many long-standing concerns for justice, peace, and the human impact on the ecosphere, recent events have forced Americans to acknowledge deep truths about our nation that are so distressing as to make one echo George Fox: "They struck at my life."[1]

I have been meditating for the last couple of weeks on this line from Isaiah 33:6: *the fear of the Lord is Zion's treasure* (NRSV).

My first response was to hear in this a challenging statement of allegiance, as in Psalm 20: *Some take pride in chariots and some in horses, but we take pride in the name of the Lord our God* (my translation of the Septuagint). This sounds to me like a call to combat, maintaining the integrity of the commonwealth of God where it has gained some being in the world and a reminder that our weapons are spiritual weapons. It is inspiring, and I have sometimes taken much encouragement from this Psalm 20 verse.

Yet, as a strategy of resistance, it does not today seem hopeful to me except as a first declaration. Resistance, if it is founded on self-assertion and rejection, is a recipe for exhaustion when the forces of Unlife are so active in so many shapes within us, among us, and around us in the culture. You see some moral outrage and respond—and even as it is beaten back, two more spring up. As when Hercules fought the Hydra, which kept sprouting heads as each was removed; or when Hercules struggled with Antaeus,[2] who drew fresh strength from every contact with the earth; or when I weed my garden and, pulling up a bunch of grass, see, alas, a stolon running off into the distance to sprout again another day . . . the labor seems relentless and multiplying. With repetition and fatigue can come an impatience, a brittleness, in which one wishes for some quick end to the struggle—and when it doesn't come, hopelessness sets in, or anger. The force of will can be depleted, no matter what one's capacity for righteous indignation may be.

But there is another way to understand the treasure of Zion that is our treasure. The "fear of the Lord" can of course mean fear as before something dangerous or threatening—but very often it can be understood as "awe," as being transported out of one's normal frame of reference. This awe, indeed, is our treasure. In that experience we are *tendered*, made vulnerable and available to growth, and we see ourselves in perspective. It is a condition in which the Light can work upon us, showing us what we are and where we stand—that is, what we are relying on at bottom. This experience can be chastening, humbling, even shocking. It is natural and easy to rely on someone or something else to be our moral compass or our source of meaning. We may discover that we have founded our hopes on what amounts to an idol, something that makes a plausible show but has not the power we have attributed to it. We invest it with our selves and lose to it some part of our individuality and our strength and, in the process, look away from truth.

But the disillusionment that comes through the working of the Light on one who has been caught in a moment of awe or awareness comes with a measure of liberation and thence some power to live into that freedom—just what has been given, no more (not yet!).

11. THE FEAR OF THE LORD

If, in the place of awe, we see the little motion of life for what it is, taste the little savor of blessing that comes with the judgment, we can make way for it to be integrated in us, incarnated in mind, heart, and habitus, and so we are grown up a little more in the life of Christ.

In a way, the Quaker "method" comes down to this: to see (feel, sense, *know*) when we stand at the threshold of awe, unsurprised by its humbleness and its seeming weakness (as it accommodates like a good teacher to our capacity), and to accept that gift with thanksgiving, knowing it to be the place where we can stay in safety, in integrity, and in a hope that is no fixed destination but a relationship, a process, a living process. From here, resistance to Unlife comes with love and forgiveness for its agents, even as we see ever more clearly that our safety resides in the keeping to the measure of life we have found, *which bears no evil in itself, takes its kingdom with entreaty, and keeps it by lowliness of mind.*

The citadel of our establishment, and the treasure within it, which is no cold gem but a nourishing Seed, is found here in the little sweet flowing of that life. The fear of the Lord, the treasure of Zion—it is our treasure.

Brian Drayton

12. Nurturing the Seed: To Friends in and around Berkeley

Berkeley (California) Friends Church invited me to be the speaker at their Quaker Heritage Day, which draws attenders from several meetings in the San Francisco Bay Area. Friends gave Darcy and me warm hospitality (there was even a small earthquake, a new experience for me). This April 2007 letter was circulated among Friends there and ended up being published in *Friends Bulletin*.[1]

Dear Friends,

As I have sat in the quiet since Darcy and I were with you last weekend, I have repeatedly had the sense that I was not free of the work I had come for. Through fatigue or ineptness, I believe that I failed to convey some part of what I felt I should offer. For this reason, and with a strong sense of love for and connection with you, I feel led to write a few words, as a conclusion to our time together, about ministry and the Seed's victory.

Our mission, our calling, is to offer hospitality to the active life of the living God, and so all ministry is given to help each other in this great task. We encounter this life in the place of stillness, when the many voices calling and commanding us from self, society, and culture can be set into the background and for a while, to our surprise, lose their command over our attention. In reaching to the Lord's lovely spirit, we can learn to feel our unity with others and with the creation and our love for them, and there we can be confident of receiving guidance about how to join in God's work of healing and reconciliation, creation and thanksgiving.

12. NURTURING THE SEED

The precious, little, sweet springing of that life is what we need to practice keeping our eye on, step by step, or feeling for its gentle stirring, its cool and refreshing presence, its sharp, clear truth-telling, which, as William Penn tells us, shows us our illness and provides at the same time the remedy.[2] Friends have loved to call this low, beautiful thing of potential and power the Seed. The very image of a little seed, stirring into opportunity, arouses in us the desire to nurture new growth, cultivate the ground, and remove the overburden that prevents growth towards the Light that is the source of life.

We know that the life Christ leads us towards is one of simplicity, peace, and other fruits of the Spirit, but we should help each other remember that these should not be the objects of our longing—we know too well how one or another virtue can itself become an idol, a substitute for what we truly are seeking, which is the lovely Spirit, our companion and shepherd. So, we must encourage each other to recall this simplest, basic yearning and to sharpen our eyes and ears for the least evidence of its activity and direction—and we must school ourselves to relish and savor the sense of Presence, if only for a little moment, before translating the guidance, the insight, the release into action or words.

In this way, by recalling over and over our first invitation, to "come and see" (John 1:39), and remembering that this first impulse of longing and interest is always precious and a treasure in itself, we will grow to see how much evidence of this life there are in so many things around us. The act of hospitality to the Spirit will become a growing joy.

Then, as we encounter in the Light fresh insight about where we are not yet free, where our compulsions and fears, resentments, wounds, and appetites bind us, we will be more able to look at these sorrowful things with directness and then turn from them towards the Light, which will help us so to live that the bindings lose their power. It is the resolute turning towards the Light, keeping our hands on the plow, that releases us, however hard it is, and in the choosing to turn is the cross. As we experience this process, we come to see that it is the preface to joy.

There is something majestic in the realization that, to the extent we and others come to honor that simple freeing power, it brings victory over the things in us that make for destructions large and small. The victory of that Seed's growth comes as it comes to overtop and shadow out the cruel, the angry, the hasty, or the fearful in us, and we are empowered to speak to that sweet, free, cool thing in others, activating it, perhaps, so that they can taste just a little of its delight again and long to know it better. So, we can come to the place John Woolman spoke of, where to turn ourselves and all we possess into the channel of universal love becomes the business of our lives.[3]

"Seed" also means those who are descended from the same ancestors. We have been promised that Christ is our elder brother, the firstborn of many brethren (as Paul put it in Romans 8:29). It is in living with this Seed, minding the Light that reveals it and guides us as we offer it hospitality, that we come to touch and are enabled to accept our being children of God and our kinship with Christ, who as Seed and Light is there at work in us before we even know how to name the power that is searching and soothing us, calling and comforting.

We minister truly, we truly serve, when we wait to feel that life, and the love that we have come to feel for it, when we speak or act. Our ministry may take the form of telling what has been done for us by that power or what others have experienced; or, it may take the form of guidance or warning about the path of growth and inward hospitality. True ministry will take as many forms as the needs are and as the messengers are. But let us help each other to practice whatever helps us come to that place of Presence and companionship, to form and hold a clear and intimate sense

12. NURTURING THE SEED

of that precious Seed, the Life of God coming to birth and growth in ourselves and all others. More than that, let us never be too proud, or knowing, or weary to stop and give thanks for that simple, sweet Presence, the foundation and goal of our soul's life.

In Christian love, your friend,

Brian Drayton

> He is no true minister of Jesus Christ, but [he] who is led forth by His Spirit; and such we rejoice to hear declaring the things of God. Otherwise, upon meeting, we sit silent in the tongue, yet having a heart full of praises, where we worship God in Spirit and truth, who makes our bodies temples for the same Spirit, not speaking by hearsay and human arts, but lay all that down. When earthy thoughts, earthy words and earthy works are all laid aside and the temple within us is ready, the light of Christ shining in it, and the Lord with a further manifestation of His love enters it by His eternal power, [there]upon we can truly say that the Lord's presence is amongst us, feeding His flock and making us feel the power of an endless life.
>
> —William Britten, *Silent meetings: a wonder to the world* (1660)

13. Not to be discouraged by the great challenges before us: To New England Friends

> The concern to write this letter arose in the spring of 2016 after I attended several Friends meetings and committees.

Dear Friends:

More than once in recent weeks, someone has spoken to me of discouragement, even despair, as they confront not only the challenges that come with living a human life but also the challenges of the times. I have spoken such things to others, to myself, and to God, in the quiet. All times are challenging, of course, but the nature of the interlocking systems constructed by, for, or against the more than seven billion people on earth, combined with the wounds and gifts of history and the intricate, beyond-human workings of the world organism, are unlike anything we have seen before.

Moreover, one consequence of our networked lives is that we can hear both the great cries of anguish and the subtle hints of unfolding disarray—perhaps the judgment coming upon us of our social heedlessness and individual inertia or our unfaithfulness by omission. In any case, I am very aware that I am one among many who feels burdened and at the same time called to understand how to live freely, faithfully, hopefully, and truthfully in my time.

In this connection, I have been reflecting recently on this quotation from George Fox's *Journal*:

> For the Lord had said unto me if I did but set up one in the same spirit that the prophets and apostles were in that gave forth the Scriptures, he or she

13. NOT TO BE DISCOURAGED

should shake all the country in their profession ten miles about them.[1]

When I quoted this in a recent gathering, people chuckled at the small scale of the impact Fox had envisioned—ten miles! Amazing! Quaint! But as I have thought of it over the past few weeks, I find here another tool for addressing the corrosive "spirit of the times"— not the only tool, nor maybe the best tool, but one I need to use to better effect: "not to be more than God would have you be." This can be understood as a counsel of Quietism and disengagement, but I do not think that is correct.

After all, the Friends who gave such counsel felt they were part of a new phase of God's world-transforming work, Christ come again in the bodies of his saints. But they were also aware of the facts of incarnation, the partial knowledge that comes with finitude, and the way that our power and our testimony are limited by our divided selves, our many-mindedness, and our temptation to claim what we can envision or can know intellectually but not embody or realize in our life, in our living, acting, perceiving, hoping.

Yet, still they longed for and expected revolution, a top-to-bottom reconstitution of individuals and societies with its motive power and its direction coming from the God who sent the prophets, working through the spirit called Christ, our shepherd, pathfinder, and teacher. They witnessed just such an "overturning" that we, oppressed by possible futures and global news, long for— out of compassion (which strengthens) as much as out of anxiety (which weakens).

Fox's "ten miles" reminds me to bring into my meditations on concern and action the recognition that my awareness of the global crisis does not equip me to act on a global scale, and *it does not require me to do so.*

I must see as widely as I can and work to understand what my part is—at this moment—in the whole. When John Wilhelm Rowntree prayed, "Lay on us the burden of the world's suffering,"[2] he certainly did not mean, "Put the Society of Friends in charge of solving the world's problems."

Rather, I understand his words to mean: "Let us see the world as it is, not as we experience it in our favored condition or our little sector of the great globe. Let us not be content with a cheap response to the Ocean of Darkness. In our measure, we have experienced how the Ocean of Light can flow over it, and we are confident in that power, but we know that there is much more growth ahead and that in that growth there is "much to die to," as Job Scott said.[3] Help us see ever more truly, O Spirit of Truth; O Spirit of Love, help us not deny your promptings in our heart; O craftsman God, help us turn our hands to the work that you set before us to do in our time. God of abundance, who yet counts each sparrow and seed as precious, help us walk under your guidance into fulness of engagement, greatness of heart, and our full measure as partners in your ministry of reconciliation and healing!"

Brian Drayton

14. Friends, welcome prophets among us in these dark times! To New England's Meetings

> Many of us were discouraged by the results of the November 2016 election and were seeking how to respond in a way that was grounded in the Spirit and could speak or witness prophetically to the love of God. I wrote this letter in December 2016. The first stirrings of a witness come in an individual who has been opened to a concern. In the early stages, such a concern may need careful cultivation so that what is good in it can emerge. It may well not be easily recognizable.

Dear Friends,

Many of us are feeling under the weight of grief, fear, and anger in the face of national and world events. Many of us are digging deep to feel where a prophetic response may be. Is there a word from the Lord that Friends are to carry at this time, in deed or in word? Is our spiritual condition healthy, alert, and clear enough to hear and receive such a word?

Here is one thing I know: a prophetic people is one that welcomes the arising of prophecy. The first motion is, in love, to make room for the leadings and the people who are led and give them opportunity to bring what they have been given. This advice comes from the earliest life of the Christian movement.

In the ancient book of advice called the *Didache* or *The Teaching of the Twelve Apostles*,[1] the little fellowships gathered in Christ's name are admonished to be open to the motion of the Spirit as embodied in traveling ministers: "Let every apostle [one who has been sent] who comes to you be received as the Lord." Knowing that we have this treasure in earthen vessels, we are to "try the spirits" and feel where the divine is present when someone feels moved to act or speak under the guiding influence of the Divine Spirit—but we are warned not to quench the Spirit's motion but to accept the unexpected activity of that Spirit in our lives as a community as well as individuals: *The Spirit blows where it will, and you hear its sound but don't know whence it comes or whither it goes. So is everyone who is born of the Spirit* (John 3:8).

As a people, we have fallen so far into a comfortable and secular mind that we think concerns and leadings are somehow a matter personal to the concerned Friend and our meetings can pick and choose whom to hear, whom to invite and allow to come among us! That is a way to avoid the uncomfortable evidence that the living God is still working through us, preparing individuals and pushing them or drawing them into service. It is a way not to change, not to grow, and to keep control of our schedules and our attention—to keep ourselves unfree. We often talk about being "spirit-led," but as a people how available are we really to that experience?

When we make time for the unexpected, when we accept the opportunities that come to us through Friends who are called to travel to us and have the encouragement of their meetings to do so, we enable those Friends, and others not yet arisen, to learn better how to watch for, hear, bear, and accomplish their service. Our meetings are "schools of the prophets"—or can be if we recognize the opportunities that come our way, accept them with joy, and learn from them—both from the message and from our experience of reception and discernment.

I have known many Friends, newly drawn into service, who have been discouraged by the convention that prophets come to meetings only when meetings issue invitations. This turns the matter upside down, Friends. The calling and the service are given through the body, through and out of the common life in the Spirit, and represent an invitation from God to see, to feel, to know, and perhaps to act in fresh ways,

14. FRIENDS, WELCOME PROPHETS

in ways renewed by the living water of God's life that brings these leadings and opportunities to us.

It can be inconvenient for a meeting to make room for such an unplanned "wildcat" experience of the Spirit. It may also be that a Friend's concern brought to a meeting will require some discernment by the meeting about ways and means. I can assure you, though, that it is pretty inconvenient for a Friend to have such a concern, to set aside other things, and to dare to stand forth, to dare to speak for God and for us. The sense of unreadiness, of unworthiness, of emptiness is very sharp in such a Friend, and they are only too conscious of difficulties for themselves and for those they visit. Yet the act of faithfulness, however imperfectly accomplished, is a step into greater life, and if it is rooted in love, it is evidence of God's work and life active among us. And, Friends, there is such a famine among us, and among people in general, for such evidence!

So, if a Friend reaches out to your meeting with an earnest statement that they are traveling under a concern with the unity of their meeting (your brothers and sisters!), remember that we can earn a prophet's reward even by offering a cup of water to a prophet. Find a way to entertain this Friend, as we are to entertain strangers sent among us, for thereby we may unexpectedly be visited by an angel—not the traveling Friend but the beloved Spirit, the Shepherd and Teacher, made available in the giving and receiving of spiritual hospitality. Make room, Friends, light your lamps in welcome, live like people who truly love the Spirit and who love to see the springs of Life break forth in any one!

In Christian love, your friend,

Brian Drayton

15. It doesn't have to be this way: Proclaiming gospel values, with a note on "original sin"

I adapted this from a message I gave in worship in June 2020, later posted on my blog, Amor Vincat.

I found myself thinking of my dad this morning. Every year, in his seventh-grade science class (in the 1960s and '70s), he'd give a lesson about life on other worlds. The kids would be engaged, of course, and at some point he'd ask: "What would you do if a flying saucer landed in your backyard and a little green man came out?" The kids would respond, "I'd run!" "I'd shoot 'em!"

My dad would strike them dumb by saying, "Not me. I'd try to talk with them." Then he'd explain why he'd want to hear what the travelers might say and intend. He'd come home and tell the story with a chuckle. In the midst of the Vietnam War fever, this was an arrestingly alternative approach—counter-cultural, you might say. My beloved, sweet father was not at all free of racial and other prejudices, but he saw the problem with prejudice and, in those years at least, responded to communitarian impulses that he thought were the best of America.

This annual seventh-grade ritual came back to me, I think, because of the recent protracted public outcry about systemic brutality against black people and the long list of injustices and outrages perpetrated against the powerless, and especially people of color, by the powerful. It's so relentless a feature of human history up to the present, like war and sexism and brutality to children and the earth, that it seems obviously to be rooted in the fiber of our being, ineradicable from human behavior. No wonder, I think, that theologians developed the doctrine of original sin, which is

15. IT DOESN'T HAVE TO BE THIS WAY

that our natures start out broken just because of who we are: sons of Adam, daughters of Eve.

No wonder George Fox found it hard going to preach freedom from sin through the power of the Light of Christ within and his opponents "roared and preached up sin," arguing that liberation was only to be found in the next life. But, as Fox was not the first to note, if *[t]here is none righteous, no, not one* (Romans 3:10, based on Ecclesiastes 7:20), then why are we continually exhorted by scriptures and preachers to live blamelessly, to strive after righteousness? What, after all, can it mean to walk in the Light, as children of the Light, if we are fundamentally hearts of darkness? What, indeed, is the "relevance of an impossible ideal"?[1] It is a cruel teaching, when Augustine and his followers tell us we have to accept it and accept that all the admonitions of the prophets and the Savior himself to cast off sin and walk in righteousness don't really mean what they say.

Now, many Friends may object, "Well, so much the worse for them, and I don't really care what Paul or Luther have to say about this stuff. All that matters is what I can say." Yet if we are worshippers of God, and that God is one, the God of Jesus and of Fox and of Paul, then somehow the teachings that we believe we receive inwardly must at least be engaged with the contrasting understandings that come apparently from the same source. After all, the often quoted "What canst thou say?" passage in Margaret Fell's account is about engaging with the Scriptures through the power of the Spirit that gave them forth:

> [Fox] stood up upon his seat or form and desired that he might have liberty to speak. And he that was in the pulpit said he might. And the first words that he spoke were as followeth: 'He is not a Jew that is one outward, neither is that circumcision which is outward, but he is a Jew that is one inward, and that is circumcision which is of the

heart'. And so he went on and said, How that Christ was the Light of the world and lighteth every man that cometh into the world; and that by this Light they might be gathered to God, etc. And I stood up in my pew, and I wondered at his doctrine, for I had never heard such before. And then he went on, and opened the Scriptures, and said, 'The Scriptures were the prophets' words and Christ's and the apostles' words, and what as they spoke they enjoyed and possessed and had it from the Lord'. And said, 'Then what had any to do with the Scriptures, but as they came to the Spirit that gave them forth. You will say, Christ saith this, and the apostles say this; but what canst thou say? Art thou a child of Light and hast walked in the Light, and what thou speakest is it inwardly from God?'[2]

But Friends saw that their understanding that God is still with us, still teaching and preaching as from the beginning when He walked in the garden with Adam and Eve, means that our imperfect hearing must recognize the following (in Isaac Penington's words):

A third great help, which in the tender mercy of the Lord I have had experience of, is sobriety of judgment. Not to value or set up mine own judgment, or that which I account the judgment of life in me, above the judgment of others, or that which is indeed life in others. For the Lord hath appeared in others, as well as to me; yea, there are others who are in the growth of his truth, and in the purity and dominion of his life, far beyond me. Now for me to set up, or hold forth, a sense or judgment of anything in opposition to them, this is out of the sobriety which is of the truth. Therefore, in such cases, I am to retire, and fear before the Lord, and wait upon him for a clear discerning and sense of his truth, in the unity and demonstration of his Spirit with others, who are of him, and see him.[3]

15. IT DOESN'T HAVE TO BE THIS WAY

Well, it just so happens that, as the world has turned and brought us to the events of June 2020, my wanderings through the Greek New Testament have brought me to Paul's great epistle to the Romans, and for fun I have been keeping Erasmus's *Annotations* and *Paraphrases* of the New Testament within reach. In Romans 5 comes the passage that serves as an important cornerstone for the idea of imputed sin, which is that we already start out at birth with a burden of sin because our forefather Adam (and foremother Eve) committed the original sin. The passage (5:12) was translated in the Latin Vulgate to suggest that sin entered the world because of Adam "in whom all have sinned"—with the implication that the sinfulness was inherited. But Erasmus pointed out that Augustine (whose Greek was admittedly limited) was the only one among the early Fathers who understood the passage this way.

The alternative is to understand the clause as meaning *since* (or *in that*) all have sinned, and Erasmus argues that the reason we have all sinned is that we are imitating our parents all the way back to Adam: "no one does not imitate the example of the first parent."[4] Sin is therefore a learned behavior—all too easy, given human nature.

But if sin is learned, it can be unlearned, though since our proclivity to sin is so great, the unlearning is only possible when we are willing to acknowledge the need and find and seek to adopt alternative responses to the occasions of sin— and seek and accept the necessary clemency and power of Christ's spirit. Christ the teacher, Dr. Logos, can diagnose and prescribe the necessary medicine. It's up to us to use it— yet God upholds us in our attempt to be faithful to the Light, both with inward help and outward help from other travelers along the way.

Quakers from the beginning have rejected the "imputed sin" idea, even as they (we) have rejected the "imputed righteousness" view of the atonement. Very many of the spiritual autobiographies of Friends, their journals, note that the authors felt that they began in innocence and that they could remember when they started to come under the bondage of sin—often all too willingly. Victorian Quakers such as Rufus Jones or John Wilhelm Rowntree were glad to embrace William Wordsworth's account of the child coming into the world "trailing clouds of glory" and only later coming under the "shades of the prison house."[5]

But if sin is learned, it can be unlearned, especially if we find or are shown alternatives so that we learn to seek and do the good and can see and recognize and live past the worse. Then, how important is the "foolishness of preaching," how important the testimony in deed and word of those who are more experienced in the journey, more practiced in the cycles of seeking, finding, and living up to (and not beyond) our measure of the Light?

It is very important that we not be silent in the face of evil. Even if all we can say is, "Things can be different! We can choose life! *This much* I have found, and *thus* have I been changed!" then we are making our contribution as citizens of the transformed realm, as children of the Light, the camp of the Lord. Faithfulness in the little (no matter how little) enables faithfulness in the greater trials. Jesus promised such growth in freedom and abundant joy in the finding of it.

16. To ministering Friends gathered in Northwest Quarterly Meeting

I have long been concerned to gather Friends active in the gospel ministry. With the minuted concurrence of Friends, I have occasionally gathered regional groups of Friends who believe they share a sustained concern for the ministry. The goal is to encourage their fellowship and mutual support and guidance. I was clear that after convening the first such gathering that I would not continue meeting with them as they should consider whether and how to continue such gatherings. But I have tried to stay in touch and hold them in prayer; sometimes letters happen, such as this one I wrote November 5, 2017, to Northwest Quarterly Meeting of New England Yearly Meeting.

Dear Friends,

I am not going to be able to join you, but have felt strongly that I wanted at least to visit by letter. I have been drawn to reflect on how we sometimes are so humble and self-effacing about our callings and the work we have done that we forget to give thanks for the evidence of life springing up in ourselves and those among whom we worship and work, to accept the reward of joy for that measure of faithfulness we have grown to. It's very important to remember that any ministry we do, if it is led, is not ours, nor is it in our own strength, but it is a part of the divine life flowing through the whole body for its health and growth. When we are rooted in that understanding, we can be freed to rejoice when we are able to lift up, encourage, or liberate that health and growth by our own participation in it and witness to it.

When we are led to and accept a share in the work of the ministry, that's the work and reward we are prepared for and commissioned to. It is no small thing to help unleash more love, more patience, more daring, more of the life and power of Christ into the world through such simple and humble means as we are given. We are called to be imaginative and ambitious in the work, abandoning ourselves to it when we feel the Spirit flowing towards and through us.

I am so grateful that you are gathering! It encourages me to see to my own watchfulness and obedience to our Teacher, who is the shepherd and guide for all who seek to serve the spiritual health of others.

    Brian Drayton

17. To Friendship Meeting

> I was invited to lead a meeting retreat for Friendship Meeting in Greensboro, North Carolina, part of North Carolina Yearly Meeting (Conservative), on the "language for the inward landscape." I was also part of an after-meeting discussion about the institution of "recorded ministers," then an active question in the meeting. While this practice is part of the yearly meeting's discipline, it is not in use in all monthly meetings. The meeting was discerning its way forward at that time. I wrote this letter December 7, 2014, to a Friend who served as an elder on behalf of the meeting for that visit.

Dear Friend,

I am very grateful for all the preparation and support the meeting undertook for my recent visit. As I have reflected on my experience since then, a few thoughts have arisen that I send you now. If they are of use, you may certainly pass them on as seems best.

The spiritual life of Friendship Meeting is rich, and it was clear that there are many open, tender, and watchful members. Though of course I was able to interact directly with only those who came to the retreat or the forum, my sense is that these were in substantial unity with the whole meeting and were earnestly concerned to uphold and care for the community.

The conversation about "recording" was about more than the narrow question of a particular historical practice, and I felt that Friends might well consider further the need for people who share a particular service to gather from time to time to hold it and each other in prayer for the work's sake and the body's. It seems to me that we come to our meeting work too often in a worldly mind in that we treat all services as if they are just assignments with little deep resonance with a Friend's gifts and callings at the time.

And what does it really mean that a person is "under the weight of a concern" or "feels a calling"? One way that I can express it is that, as a result of the secret movement and work of the Spirit in that Friend, they are particularly sensitive to a specific service—they have a growing understanding of its role in the life of the meeting or the world, a sense of how it supports other kinds of work and service, and a longing or urgency to put their hand (time, mind, energy) to some share of that work. It is both a duty and an opportunity for growth; for them, at that time, it is the opening way. The first dawning of this understanding is only a beginning; with attention and practice, more will be given, and so I have found.

The fundamental root and motive for the ministry as Friends have understood it is a motion of love, a concern for the spiritual flourishing of others, and a delight in the experience of God's presence. As John Woolman writes, "From an inward purifying and steadfast abiding under it, springs a lively operative desire for the good of others."[1]

The more a meeting welcomes this and names it as a fruit of the divine life at work among them (right here! right now!), the more Friends will be encouraged to engage in humble, free, creative, watchful, and courageous service, each according to their gifts and opportunities. It is because of the great variety of conditions, personalities, and gifts that a meeting's attention to the motions of love in individuals, and their faithful response to them, is essential if Friends are to be welcoming of the challenges the Spirit offers and to grow in the acceptance and exploration of these challenges. It's also why people who share a ministry or service are an important resource (for counsel and for comfort) to each other. One size definitely does not fit all!

17. TO FRIENDSHIP MEETING

And this, it seems to me, is more important to a meeting's witness to the world than we often recognize. Although "effectiveness" and "impact" are terms that are often spiritually harmful, and "success" in the upside-down kingdom of Christ is not what the world seeks, yet we are called to let our light shine before all that they may see our good works and glorify the divine source whose life is the root of our work. The good Samaritan *acted*.

Doing this, and making sure always to seek where the joy and love is at the heart and root of our service, we will also speak inwardly to our community—to those who are new among us, to those who are discouraged or in a dry place, and to our youth. The "speaking" will be the quality of the life they feel around them, only sometimes put into words. We will feel, and sometimes even say, hallelujah!

In Christian love, your friend,

Brian Drayton

18. For ministering Friends gathering in Plainfield

I sent this letter May 4, 2014, as an encouragement to a gathering of ministering Friends in Northwest Quarterly Meeting, whose monthly meetings are mostly located in Vermont.

Dear Friends,

You have been on my heart and mind so often in the past two weeks that I want to pay you a visit by letter since I can't join you in person. First, I want to send my love in the Spirit to you and thank you for the way you have continued to gather as you can for mutual encouragement. I eagerly follow any news I can get about you!

There is such a need among Friends—and outside Friends, too—for a ministry that is simple, loving, challenging, and consoling. Our mutual support, both when we gather and when we are apart, matters very much in helping each other keep watchful, hopeful, and energetic, each according to our gifts. It is in daily attention that our faithfulness stays lively, and it is part of the work of the ministry to keep mindful of each other as we hold in our concern the welfare of our spiritual community.

That concern for the life in the community is the underlying subject of any gathering like the one this weekend. If I were able to be present, when it was my turn to "check in" about my condition, I would share with you the question that I feel the Lord posing to me often these days: "What fruit, what harvest can you tell about? Large or small, name it in thanksgiving! Even if you only give a cup of water to a prophet, you reap a prophet's reward, so what news of

18. FOR MINISTERING FRIENDS

growth and openings? How are you using the gift I have given you?"

Most of the work of the ministry is in prayer and watchfulness, and out of that comes the readiness to get to work when the time is right. So, my answer to this challenge first must take account of how I have kept up the daily watch and how my soul fares these days, in trials and in blessings.

I can't stop there, though. Have I been on the watch for little openings of life in my Friends, or whoever I am sent to? Have I taken the opportunities I have been given to say a word of welcome, encouragement, or gratitude? There are settled Friends who may need refreshment—perhaps by com-panionship in prayer or conversation, perhaps by a word of thanks, perhaps by a suggestion, rooted in the Light, that it's time to take on a challenge suitable to their scope and experience. Time to take a risk!

After all, the call is for us all to bear fruit, each according to our kind, and to give thanks to God for it. Our treasures are for use in service, and our service should be done in reverence but also in joy. Sometimes we have to travel a ways, labor for a while, before we can feel how to inhabit the life God is giving us in both reverence *and* joy. So, we need to push, pull, comfort, ask, repair, refresh, and accompany each other in it all—just as the Spirit does with us.

We are emissaries of a God of truth, patience, abundance, compassion, freedom, and love. God baptizes us if we come even just to the brink of the living water with fire and the Holy Spirit, clarifying and amazing us!

In Christian love, your friend,

Brian Drayton

19. Building our house in the storm: A letter to New England Friends

This letter was written August 6, 2016, in advance of the 2016 annual meeting of New England Yearly Meeting.

Dear Friends,

We are gathering in Vermont to worship, work, and spend time in companionship. Yearly meeting can be such a blessed time for inquiry, growth, and consolation! In the quiet this morning, I find myself filled with gratitude because of the opportunities we have.

We will say many things about the needs of the world, and the calling we feel to respond, and the leadings we are following, and the evidence that some of us see that we are following our Guide, and the burdens we bear in our journeys.

Surely, we can say that God is at work among us and that we are trying, at least, to walk as children of the Light. In my gratitude this morning, however, one question comes with urgency: Are we taking care that our meetings are in health? Are we being faithful to the gifts that are given to help us all live close to the Wellspring of unity and our pure testimony—not of this concern or that, this "practice" or that, but the essential root, our reason for being a people at all?

All our outward doing, if it is witness—what is it a witness to? The Quaker claim is that acts of faithfulness speak of the inward life out of which they come. Recall the time when John Woolman sought to understand the origins of his concern to visit the Indians:

19. BUILDING OUR HOUSE

Twelfth of sixth month being the first of the week and a rainy day, we continued in our tent, and I was led to think on the nature of the exercise which hath attended me. Love was the first motion, and thence a concern arose to spend some time with the Indians, that I might feel and understand their life and the spirit they live in, if haply I might receive some instruction from them, or they might be in any degree helped forward by my following the leadings of truth among them.[1]

If we don't take the time to inquire where our doing comes from, to understand how *my* concern and *your* concern are rooted in the gospel life, then we can forget the grounds of our unity in the Spirit. We may find substitutes for that dear unity—with the people whose language and concerns feel most comfortable and exciting to us—but "issues loyalty" can become a reason to judge each other, a root of division.

My concern this morning is especially for those who are called to the work of ministry in all its many forms, whose purpose is to build up the community as a vessel of the divine life—in public worship or in private, in prayer or presence, in teaching or in preaching.

The work of the ministry, in all its forms, starts with listening and waiting to feel *where* the unity dwells and *what* the connections are between some present focus of concern and the whole story we as a people are acting out.

All the issues of our times are urgent, yes, but it is just as urgent that we take care that our worship and our witness are truly what we claim them to be, motions of the Spirit of Love. This has never happened except when some (many!) people have accepted their share of this work and taken concrete steps to serve and to grow in the service. What is called for from you, Friend?

Haggai was a prophet during the time of Israel's return from exile, and he was the vehicle for an urgent call, which I feel this morning is renewed to us:

> *"These people say, 'The time has not yet come to rebuild the Lord's house.'" Then the word of the Lord came through the prophet Haggai:"...You have planted much, but harvested little. You eat, but never have enough. You drink, but never have your fill. You put on clothes, but are not warm. You earn wages, only to put them in a purse with holes in it....Give careful thought to your ways. Go up into the mountains and bring down timber and build my house, so that I may take pleasure in it and be honored," says the Lord. "You expected much, but see, it turned out to be little. What you brought home, I blew away. Why?" declares the Lord Almighty. "Because of my house, which remains a ruin, while each of you is busy with your own house."* (Haggai 1:2–8 NIV)

Let's be about the building! I think it starts with a renewal of our praying, which is the workshop of all ministry.

Wait until we feel we are at the Center, and then in that confidence ask, Am I just worshipping myself, or my longings and needs? We may feel convicted then, but there comes with the judgment the gift of freedom and an opening to a clearer view of the true Center. There, we can wait in God's patience and compassion until all our certainties are overturned, and we can continue seeking until the Love comes, which can be felt when certainties are gone, and our notions are taken from us, and we have felt the poverty of our own spirits. Then the blessing comes.

It is in that poverty that we can accept the gift of the common life, the unity that Jesus testified to and prayed for, just before Gethsemane and the cross, and that has been renewed again and again thereafter. You have tasted it,

19. BUILDING OUR HOUSE

maybe! Then you know what Paul meant when he wrote (1 Corinthians 2:16): *But we have the mind of Christ.*

Brian Drayton

20. "That of God in every one": Can we not say a little more?

I published this on my blog, Amor Vincat, for Friends around the time of the 2020 New England Yearly Meeting, which was held virtually owing to the coronavirus pandemic.

Friends meetings, in making statements on a variety of social issues, often found their rationale upon the assertion that the divine Light is accessible to everyone, typically citing as our core belief that "there is that of God in every one." This article of faith is so widely cited that it is rare for us to question its use or what we actually mean by it. In what follows, *I do not suggest that we stop using it!* However, in this yearly meeting season, with minutes and epistles being crafted and circulated, I'd like to encourage Friends to examine what this phrase actually means for them and to also suggest that we can't rely on this alone as the theological basis for our social witness. Can't we say a little more?

"That of God"—what can it mean?

It sometimes seems that when Friends say "there is that of God in every one," it is really meant as the equivalent of a statement that "each individual is of value and has inalienable rights." This is a valuable thing to say, and I have no objection to it, as far as it goes. I would claim, however, that if it means this and no more, then it is really not a theological statement at all, that is, it is not a statement that reflects in any obvious way our experience of the living God. It is a sentiment that is well suited to a pluralistic democracy or as a universal statement on human rights. To claim that individuals must be treated with equal respect before the law and have equitable access to the necessities of life (including

20. "THAT OF GOD IN EVERY ONE"

those that make culture and society possible) is a liberal and just sentiment.

But do we Friends bring God into our statements out of habit? If so, then this invocation of the Deity seems more like other conventional references to God that decorate political documents and public expressions than an indication of some imperative that drives us, that is rooted in our spiritual life.

I am not comfortable to remain at that level when using the phrase. Perhaps a further exploration of what we intend by the phrase might help bring other meanings of it to the surface, and these might in turn enhance the richness of our witness and our search.

Traditionally, this statement grew out of the Quaker understanding of the nature of our relationship with God. Early Friends did not understand the word "that" in the phrase to mean a piece of God, a little private God or particle separate from the rest. In fact, you could say that the best way to unpack the phrase is to realize that there is a story attached to it. Though George Fox said it one way and Robert Barclay another, the basic idea is that God maintains an active presence, a point of contact with everyone, that has the potential to serve as a beachhead or foothold from which the Spirit can undertake its work of transformation and liberation. This "that" does mark each of us as a child of God so that we have that irreducible value and "right" to just treatment.

Yet there is something more. This "that" is a witness for the Light and against the darkness. It is from our attention to this witness that we come to learn our condition and see how to make room for the growth of the divine life in us. It is therefore a living, dynamic thing, not just an "endowment" or owner's mark. The process is part of the gift, and to acknowledge the gift we must take action, wrestle for the blessing.

- We have to live so as to cherish this birth in us. John Woolman writes, "As cherishing the spirit of love and meekness is our duty, so to avoid those things which they know works against it is a duty also." He adds, "To labor for an establishment in divine love where the mind is disentangled from the power of darkness is the great business of man's life."[1]

- This "that" shows us where next to move ourselves and offers us the ability to do so. In seeking to act so as to preserve and encourage that divine life in its growth in us and to reach to it in others, we are then also taught to see what is next to be changed in ourselves in order to continue in our service.

- We have seasoned our actions so as to reach the witness in others. What does it mean, to "answer that of God"? The life of God in us is the source of our impulses and capacities to love, to act in mercy, to distinguish light from darkness. The Seed of Christ is present inwardly, and so the arising of the savior is an experience possible for all. We cannot take for granted that our impulses are grounded in love, so our discipline should help us wait till we can touch that source and season our witness with it.

- This Seed is the ultimate source of unity among humans because the Light is one. Standing in the Light, we can see the unity. George Fox put it this way: "As people come into subjection to the spirit of God, and grow up in the image and power of the Almighty, they may receive the Word of wisdom, that opens all things, and come to know the hidden unity in the Eternal Being."[2]

What else? Some of this is "Quaker theology," but some of it is our inheritance—or participation in—the prophetic messages from Amos through Jesus and down to our own time (Thus saith the Lord). We must claim all of this and *make sure that our witness is not impoverished by not doing so.*

20. "THAT OF GOD IN EVERY ONE"

Furthermore, to both know and declare these dimensions of our witness to the world enriches our own understanding of the pervasiveness of our religious commitment and enriches also our understanding of how particularly it is that "all of life is sacred." As humans, our call is to see and name the sacredness at the heart of it all; we should not just say it is sacred but enact it with the materials of our lives.

Experience is our watchword, our traveling into all the nooks and crannies of life, and our meeting the divine life at work there. This has led to other commitments that are part of our prophetic schooling and our proclamation. Examples of this might be

> • *religious practice as a direct transaction under God's direction*: refusal of notional ceremonies and imposed religious performances. The vitality, the truthfulness of our worship is inseparable from our social witness;

> • *justice as obedience and gratitude*: the persistent cry of the prophets that all must have equitable access to the good things offered us all by God and be free from human interference in our faithful living, as well as God's preference for the poor, the excluded, and the needy;

> • *gospel order*, in relationships and in the "right use of the creatures," is integrated with qualities such as simplicity, honesty, directness, and mercy.

The core of all this is the prophetic experience when someone can say: I have seen, felt, heard God, and this is what God requires of us. Or, "The spirit of Christ by which we are guided is not changeable."[3] Can we not bring ourselves to say something more than the minimum, to hint at the power that lies in the beloved phrase "that of God"? If you have lived it even for a moment, you know the joy and freedom which that Life gives! That's part our witness, too, and part of the gift we can share when we invite others to come into the silent assemblies of God's people and join in God's construction of the "commonwealth of heaven."

21. Unity, disunity, diversity or Some mysteries of the Holy Spirit's LIFE at work in its body's members hinted at: A letter to New England Friends

New England Yearly Meeting is dynamic and theologically very diverse. Since our first gathering in 1661, we have had disagreements and, a few times, separations large and small. We have mostly learned how to maintain or regain love and unity over the years, but there are times when in the midst of laboring we are not sure what our condition is. Will love win out again? Can we still trust the Spirit to bring us into clarity? I wrote and distributed this letter in August 2007 at such a time. It was later published with a helpful introduction by Hugh Barbour.[1]

Dear Friends,

I am writing this letter at a time when Friends are experiencing another moment when their disunity is strongly felt, when discord and divergence seem prominent characteristics of our fellowship. We have drifted into a chronic state of disunity, which is damaging to our decisions and to the quality of our worship together. I believe, however, that this disunity has remarkably little to do with the diversity of belief and doctrine and shared or unshared history that so often occupies our attention. I have come to understand that unity is not a product but a process and that 'living in unity' is another way to describe the watchful life that is the heart of Friends' response to the presence of the inward Teacher. When we feel disunity, therefore, we are recognizing the effects of a break in the flow of the divine life within and among us. Carefully worded minutes, statements of purpose, and actions of witness can all be serviceable at such times, but only if they arise from a renewed acquaintance with the Holy Spirit, even as we are in the midst of our trouble.

We are so desirous of unity and peace among ourselves that any hint of discord causes us pain and alarm. When we feel that bonds of mutual understanding have been painfully broken, we long for their restoration and we throw ourselves into anxious search and intense discussion. The sense of distance and alienation arouses fear and sorrow. Naturally enough, the consequences of fear and grief are produced and shared, each of us bringing forth a sample from our inward treasury of spiritual substance—materials that may be constructive, destructive, doubtful, or committed, according to our condition. Our contributions then have their consequences, and every one of us who is teachable learns important lessons about their allegiances and their limits, and what they actually put their faith in. But damage has been done, and in the life of a society the pain of old wounds can persist for generations, affecting the ideas and behavior of people who did not participate in the original events and who may have no traceable personal tie to actual participants. Such is the amplifying effect of society and of belonging, the locating of oneself in a story that started long before one's own existence.

In this letter to my dear Friends, I want to explore some aspects of unity and disunity among us. I will draw on two incidents from Friends history to explore some characteristics of disunity and of unity and suggest not some solutions but indications of a path forward—in the very midst of our diversity.

I. Beyond the cliché of disunity

> Do I contradict myself?
> Very well, then I contradict myself.
> I am large, I contain multitudes.
>
> —Walt Whitman, *Song of Myself*, 1855

21. UNITY, DISUNITY, DIVERSITY

It is common enough for us Friends to tell each other that we shouldn't be upset at the disunity we are feeling, that it's been an integral part of the movement from the beginning. For example, in the middle of the "realignment" debate in Friends United Meeting more than twenty-five years ago,[2] William P. Taber wrote:

> I have some observations about differences among Friends. The first one is rather obvious. There have always been differences among Friends, from the very beginning. Historians generally note that there were four separations during George Fox's lifetime.[3]

There is a certain cold comfort in this insight, of course, but the ease with which we repeat it, true though it is, disguises another part of the truth, which is that we have also known unity from the beginning and, indeed, the feeling of being drawn into oneness has been a powerful reason for hope and commitment to the truth as held by Friends.

The early Friends spoke almost ecstatically about their experience of God at work among them and gathering them into one. George Fox, in his Pendle Hill vision, saw "a great people to be gathered," but the people themselves described the experience of being gathered.

One of the most famous accounts is Francis Howgill's remembrance as part of his memorial to Edward Burrough, his longtime yoke-mate in the ministry:

> [T]he Kingdom of Heaven did gather us, and catch us all, as in a net, and his heavenly power at one time drew many hundreds to land. We came to know a place to stand in and what to wait in; and the Lord appeared daily to us, to our astonishment, amazement, and great admiration, insomuch that we often said one unto another with great joy of heart: 'What, is the Kingdom of God come to be with men? And will he take up his tabernacle among the sons of men, as he did of old? Shall

> we, that were reckoned as the outcasts of Israel, have this honor of glory communicated among us, which were but men of small parts and of little abilities, in respect of many others, as amongst men?
>
> And from that day forward, our hearts were knit unto the Lord and one unto another in true and fervent love, in the covenant of Life with God; and that was a strong obligation or bond upon all our spirits, which united us one unto another. We met together in the unity of the spirit, and of the bond of peace, treading down under our feet all reasoning about religion. And holy resolutions were kindled in our hearts, as a fire, which the Life kindled in us to serve the Lord while we had a being, and mightily did the Word of God grow amongst us, and the desires of many were after the Name of the Lord. O happy day! O blessed day! the memorial of which can never pass out of my mind. And thus the Lord, in short, did form us to be a people for his praise in our generation."[4]

New England Friends, too, have experienced moments in which we were so covered by the sense of God's presence that we felt ourselves in a transcendent interconnection. More than once during our yearly meeting sessions over the years, I have been reminded of this passage from Fox's *Journal* reporting on his own attendance at a general meeting in New England in 1672:

> [W]hen it was ended it was hard for Friends to part, for the glorious power of the Lord which was over all and his blessed Truth and life flowing amongst them had so knit and united them together that they spent two days in taking leave of one another and Friends went away being mightily filled with the presence.[5]

Our experience of these times should make us alert to the complexity of the meeting's inner life and also to the nature of unity in the Spirit. Such moments, in which we experience an improbable freedom and clarity, can come at times when

21. UNITY, DISUNITY, DIVERSITY

the meeting has been painfully aware of disagreement among its members, when business meetings or even social times seem laborious or tense. Recently, a Friend recounted to me a difficult clearness committee in which members of a meeting who were strongly at odds took time to worship together. My friend recalled with some astonishment that there was a solid feeling of God's presence, tender and healing. The people present had been expressing their grievances with each other heatedly, and afterwards there was no miraculous closing of wounds; yet all agreed on this, that they had been granted a period of grace that they yearned to live back into if only they could find a way there. No one present felt that the sense of covering was a lie. Such stories are precious and not rare.

These sweet moments in which we feel ourselves closely drawn together are every bit as important as the times when we feel at odds and alienated or see no way to move forward from some painful dilemma. They teach us that unity is not a cognitive experience, though we cannot separate our minds from our spirits or our bodies. When Jesus prayed (John 17:21) that his friends be made one, and one with him, and through him one with God, he could not have been speaking about their speaking in intellectual unison, something Jesus did not require of his friends and disciples at any point in his ministry.

By the same token, disunity is not primarily an intellectual condition but something much more complex. It is a condition that most often has incubated for a long period of time and can remain at a low level of intensity for a long period of time before it becomes visible and formidable.

I remember one summer in my youth when a brush fire flared up in my town in Maine. The volunteer fire department came out, but the fire covered so large an area of woods and ledges that a call for extra volunteers went out. While the hottest part of the fire was fought by people who knew what they were doing, I joined the cleanup crew, gleaning, as it were, in the fields that had already been harvested by the moving flames. With an "Indian pump" on my back, I patrolled my allotted area, looking for hot spots in the turf and soaking them down. The experienced men told us how embers left behind by the fire could smolder for weeks in the litter, too starved for air to flame out but kept alive and hot enough that a little change in the weather—a higher wind, a few weeks' drought—could enable the hidden coals to strengthen and burst out into a blaze that could scorch the landscape again.

So it is with disunity. At a low level it can be cooking along, unnoticed if we are not watching for it but ready to leap out when the conditions are right. We find ourselves acting defensively, and our patience runs out quickly. The connection rooted in the Life has been lost—and then it becomes all too easy to find intellectual and historical reasons that seem to justify the rift. Yet, these were not the cause of the disunity, though they can become fuel for its persistence.

Diversity and disagreement are not the same as disunity, and there is no reason why they should not coexist with unity. There have been many points, both in the past and in the present, when diversity has characterized our Society but disunity has not. Diversity can be problematic, confusing, and distracting; sometimes it can be based upon fallacy or mistake. Yet, it can also be a source of creativity and growth. Which way it affects us depends on how we live with it and whether we are maintaining love and unity as a people.

To explore some aspects of disunity, I would like to raise up two events in Quaker history in which unity was broken and then restored. One was occasioned by an individual, and the other was rooted in different visions of Quakerism that became embodied in hostile groups. We are well aware of both kinds of disunity in our own day and realize that they are often not strictly separable; disunity arising because of an individual can have consequences that involve the whole group, and groups at odds are made up of individuals. Yet the distinction has some practical use in thinking about division and reunion.

II. Disunity arising around an individual: James Nayler

From time to time, it happens that a person will appear so clearly to embody hitherto diffuse issues or differences that willy-nilly a division springs up around them and their defenders and detractors are led into disunity.

We have seen in our own yearly meeting, and in our monthly meetings, how differing judgments in the body about a particular person's words or deeds result in partisan tensions. Sometimes the focal person is seen to represent a long-standing grievance, which now can be identified and made a point requiring decision; sometimes, the person acts or speaks in a way that causes pain or consternation, and then loyalty or some other sense of connection makes it necessary for others to take the person's part, defending them against censure or other reaction from those who judge them to be in the wrong. The person becomes a symbol of something larger. Difference or disagreement can become disunity at this transition when stakes are seen to be higher and choices gain new implications.

This accretion of meanings, which leads to a gain in intensity or emotional heat, is evidence that something else was going on before, that differences and disaffections of other kinds had been accumulating. Perhaps these differences and disaffections had not been recognized as such, or they had been seen and named by some but left unattended or discounted. The gestation of distrust prepares it to come forth under some invitation or pretext—but already the damage is being done, and the precipitating event is not a cause but the beginning of a fulfillment.

I have been writing in generalities, because to write about events we have all lived through recently may bring forward too much detail, too much residue of disunity, defensiveness, judgment, and the main point may be lost, which is this: in our daily watch, we must be on the lookout for such accumulations of difference and distance because in them already the unity of the body is under assault and the discernment that may be called for when a problem arises is being undercut.

So, let us recall the case of James Nayler, that magnetic figure from early Quakerism. After four years of increasing success as a leader of the Quaker movement, Nayler joined the Quaker campaign in London in 1655. With his fervent and vulnerable spirit, quick mind, eloquent tongue, and intense application, Nayler found himself fully deployed in public debate and preaching and private counsel and guidance to the movement's new adherents in the capital. When other stalwarts such as Francis Howgill and Edward Burrough were called to labor elsewhere later in the year, Nayler stayed on, for several months the most prominent and solitary Publisher of Truth in the intense arena of the great city of London.

Fatigue set in, and in its train some darkening of mood. Though James stayed in epistolary contact with his brothers and sisters in the work, he was paradoxically isolated in the midst of throngs. Support and encouragement, praise and appreciation came from a small coterie of men and women who felt especially reached by Nayler—whether by the way he preached the Quaker gospel, or by his presence and personality. Inspired and stirred up, they not only helped him in a time of weakness but they also spoke explicitly of ways in which he surpassed other leaders—and the comparing mind's eye turned most swiftly and naturally to George Fox.

When Nayler was at last given a chance to leave town and visit his Yorkshire home for a respite, tensions arose between

21. UNITY, DISUNITY, DIVERSITY

people identified most closely with him and those allied with the weight of the leadership. When Nayler refused to rebuke or judge those who saw themselves as his partisans, maintaining the possibility that they might be responding to the Spirit's promptings, he unintentionally was associated with their statements, their boisterous pugnacities, and their reproaches against the Quaker "establishment."

The disruptive behavior of some partisans elicited increasingly strong condemnations and demands for change from the movement's leaders. Under these warnings, and especially in coming months as Fox exerted his authority, Nayler found in himself questions, wounds, resentments, and a sense of rivalry. Beyond this, though, there was the largely unspoken debate happening in the minds and souls of the leaders about the balance between individual leadings and corporate testimony. Such large theological issues, wrapped up also with interpersonal tensions, were intensified—both in importance and in urgency—by the persecutions that the leaders of the movement, including Fox and Nayler, were experiencing.

Most recountings of the "Nayler episode" culminate in the "sign" enacted by Nayler and his followers in Bristol and the subsequent savage punishment of Nayler followed by his later reconciliation with Friends.[6] But for Friends now, in New England, we must pause for a lesson drawn from the period before the final crisis.

Here is a charismatic and vulnerable leader, a complex personality undergoing inward crises and increasingly unable to discern his own condition, the conditions of those around him, and the way he should take forward. At a time when his own clarity is clouded by bodily fatigue, personal doubts, and a dawning sense of disharmony with his closest associates, he becomes a rallying point, a catalyst, which speeds and intensifies reactions within his community.

The thing I wish to emphasize is that the materials enabling the fractures and divisions that later became visible had been gathering for some time. Distrust and misunderstanding, resentment and anger, fear and confusion—all often directed towards oneself as well as others—were already present. Diversity of voice, of view, and of experience had been present from the beginning, perhaps hard to see in the blinding sense of the Light powerfully at work. Like the germ in a seed, disunity was present at a low level, and conditions nurtured it so that it grew into damaging maturity.

The disunity was not centered in the disharmony of ideas or experience, of expression or mood. It gained its potency from the attachment of difference to personalities followed by judgment so that the question more and more became "Who is right?" (and therefore who should have preference) rather than "What is right?" or, in the terms of Quaker spirituality, "Does Truth prosper? Where does the Seed suffer, where is it coming under oppression?"

A Poison Tree

I was angry with my friend:
I told my wrath, my wrath did end.
I was angry with my foe:
I told it not, my wrath did grow.

And I water'd it in fears,
Night & morning with my tears;
And I summoned it with smiles,
And with soft deceitful wiles.

And it grew both day and night,
Till it bore an apple bright;
And my foe beheld it shine,
 And he knew that it was mine,

And into my garden stole
When the night had veil'd the pole:

21. UNITY, DISUNITY, DIVERSITY

> In the morning glad I see
> My foe outstretch'd beneath the tree.
>
> —William Blake, 1794

To a remarkable extent, unity was re-established among the early Friends, and it happened because of work at several levels. Nayler himself did the most important work because he spent his first months in prison reflecting on the path that had led to Bristol, to disunity, and to torment. As he explored events, his focus on the divine life in himself and in others provided a point of reference and a source of judgment that was not partisan. He saw that he had been distracted and had allowed himself to be led not by the tender and truthful spirit of Christ but by others' enthusiasms, passions, and needs. He was not willing to judge or examine them in the Light in the way he was willing to judge and examine himself (or, rather, allow the Light to examine him). Thus, when differences and disagreements arose, he was not established in that Light, which would have allowed him to see where his critics were right and also where they were in the wrong; he was not able to speak with the accents of the Light to that of God in himself or in them. When he understood why he had reacted as he did and felt again the sense that God had not left him, even though he had wandered from God, then he was able to acknowledge his own fault and reach out to those he had wounded, misled, or rejected before and endure the hard work of reconciliation. He wrote "to the Life of God in all":

> [A]ll you in whom any measure of this precious Life has been betrayed, either through this or any other thing . . . to the light thereof you may return in yourselves, and there wait till the Life arise, which is your return, and which must give you rest with the flock of God; for it's the Life that's the door and the fold, and without it you will be but wanderers, and lost in all your thoughts and motions. . . .

> [T]ake heed of evil thoughts to which you will be tempted, you that are gone out from the true light, or an evil eye going out of your own hearts against the truth you were once called into, or them that walk in it, to spy faults in others and feed thereon; this food will but strengthen the enmity in you against you and your return, and with this you may make bonds which you cannot break. . . .
>
> And this I am moved to warn you of, having been often tempted therewith, that the Life of peace and truth may only live and guide in you in all, without which there can be no true unity with God or His people.[7]

But Nayler's great work of repentance and clarification would not perhaps have been enough if similar work were not going on elsewhere in the body of Friends (the body of the people, in whom the Spirit makes its appearance). A leader in this work was William Dewsbury, who persistently kept his eye on the Life and Seed at work and spoke to it in Fox and in Nayler, whose reconciliation would signal a repair (however imperfect) between these two central witnesses to the Quaker message. This focus is seen in words Dewsbury wrote on an earlier occasion to Judge Thomas Fell,

> Friend, that which calls for purity in thee is dear to me, and with it I suffer, which often secretly groans in thee for deliverance. And whilst thou lend thy ear to the pure counsel of the holy Seed, thou art almost persuaded to lay thy crown in the dust at the feet of Christ . . . and to follow him daily in the cross. . . . To the pure light of Christ in thy conscience I speak, which will witness me.[8]

In similar tones, he wrote to Nayler:

> What hath been done in the hour of temptation, out of the light, let the light and life judge it out; that in the light and life of our God, the whole body grow in the unity of the Spirit, to bear one another, serve one another, build up one another; that amongst all, not any master be, but Christ, our head.[9]

III. Disunity appearing as a movement: The Wilkinson–Story separation

In the 1670s, during the time of the greatest persecutions Friends ever encountered, George Fox led the first and most creative period of development of the discipline. He was powerfully convinced that faithfulness to the ordering power of the gospel was leading to the setting up of the meeting structure, the institution of women's meetings, and many other features of Quaker practice in worship and behavior. The importance of corporate discernment and its use to balance individual guidance and individual dissent from the Truth had grown with successive internal crises and also in response to the decimation of the charismatic leaders who had gathered the children of the Light and nurtured the movement that ensued.[10]

Fox spent himself tirelessly in person and in letters to articulate these ordering aspects of Quaker culture and to persuade Friends around the country to adopt them. Meetings of ministers at the yearly meeting and quarterly meeting levels issued directives that amounted to embryonic rules of discipline. Unlike earlier such statements, such as the Letter of the Elders of Balby (1656),[11] however, these now carried force not only because of the spiritual authority of the authors but also because of institutional structures that were taking shape and creating the Religious Society of Friends out of the Quaker movement.

In 1673, two of the first Publishers of Truth, John Wilkinson and John Story, became the most visible objectors to some of the new arrangements—and perhaps, beyond any particulars, to the whole thrust of the move towards institutionalization.[12] Some of the objections sound self-serving. For example, the dissidents were not sure it was necessary that Friends should always hold their meetings in public at a time of danger and argued that perhaps it was rightly ordered to lay low sometimes. And, while they held with the Quaker testimony against the paying of tithes, they wanted to leave this choice to the individual conscience since the fines and distraints that resulted from such law-breaking could ruin a family.

Other objections of the dissenters seem different in kind. Women's meetings might be useful in big cities, where there was a lot of poor relief and other pastoral work appropriate to women, but elsewhere such separate meetings for business were superfluous. The Story/Wilkinson dissenters did not approve of people groaning and vocalizing in meetings while Friends were preaching. They did not like the requirement that Friends issue "papers of condemnation" of those who misbehaved unless the disorderly Friend themself wished to acknowledge wrongdoing in this way.

Behind and around these particulars, however, one feels clearly that the objecting Friends felt an encroaching corporatism that was cramping the movement of the Spirit and the freedom of conscience that are central to the Quaker testimony. When the leaders insisted that these measures of discipline were needed to maintain love and unity among Friends, the dissenters retorted that the result was not a real unity but rather a counterfeit "Foxonian-unity," the result of external coercion. There is a certain irony in this since one effect of Fox's organizational work at this time was to make himself dispensable. (Ralph Waldo Emerson might suggest that the institution of Quakerism is the lengthened shadow of the man Fox, but to a remarkable extent this is not how things turned out, and Fox's own work is a major reason.[13]) Yet, at the time, the move to the discipline was resisted in part because it was so strongly identified with Fox's leadership.

The accusations and condemnations that flew back and forth reveal that in this case, as in the Nayler case, the open debates were the manifestation of an inner dissonance that had been at work for some time. Both sides condemned the other's behaviors, words, attitudes, and motives. In between

21. UNITY, DISUNITY, DIVERSITY

moved people such as Isaac Penington, who saw that reasonable spiritual concerns lay on both sides and who hoped that each party could see the good with the bad. Dewsbury wrote that he longed for God to

> subject all convinced of His truth to throw down their crowns of self-striving before His throne, that in his ancient love all may be buried that is not of His nature, and in Him all bound up in the unity of His spirit; that the Lord may be one, His name one; that all may be restored that hath been in any measure serviceable in the hand of the Lord and not that any be lost that have tasted of His goodness.[14]

Friends on both sides (including Fox) acknowledged the importance of the dissidents' concerns about overregulation of the Spirit's operation in the individual, but the sense of the Life present was not strong enough to overcome personal and ideological wounds. Yet, the debates continued at the level of the outward and resulted in a separation in some meetings. The dissident meetings died away in a few years, and a few of their adherents rejoined the main movement.

IV. 'Divers liveries': Personality can appear to be revelation

> The humble, meek, merciful, just, pious and devout souls are everywhere of one religion; and when death has taken off the mask, they will know one another, though the divers liveries they wear here make them strangers.
>
> —William Penn, *Some Fruits of Solitude*

We have learned through sometimes painful discernment that the Spirit's workings in us can be hard to recognize. Friends are very aware that earlier stages of our spiritual paths continue to influence us, often for the rest of our lives. We also are aware that the struggles and discoveries of others can be full of instruction for ourselves, and so the stories of exploration, of seeking, mistaking, experimenting, and finding, are respected as evidence of the spiritual life, truthful despite all the diversity, and deeply related in the Spirit, even as we struggle to put words to what is shared.

We see in the two Quaker stories sketched above that it is nothing new to make the great mistake of assuming that something or someone that arouses strong feelings in us is by that very fact a kind of revelation. When we see a person passionately advocating a position or hear a trenchant critique of a custom or regulation in our community, it is tempting to feel that these matters are signals of a fresh opening, a prophetic crack in the normal, which will open the way to greater knowledge, greater liberation, greater spiritual events. The advocates—which may be we ourselves or others whom we are drawn to support—are transformed into symbols, avatars, message-bearers. Their cause, their grievance, their new word, and their rejection become matters of grave importance because of the meanings that are attributed to them.

It is curious how often a meeting can season, pray over, and learn about an issue and then reach unity on a minute, and yet this can be ignored as irrelevant by meeting members rather than being seen as evidence of the Spirit working among us, making use of our careful processes to guide us into greater faithfulness. Yet a person or group with a grievance or an exciting new idea can galvanize members, engage them as partisans pro or con, and stir up the most intense conviction that the Spirit is at work—perhaps evidenced by the passion of the innovators, perhaps by the resistance of those who do not accord with them.

The important point here is that we can take or mistake many kinds of things as revelations, but, whether they are embodied in a person's vision or in a movement or in an institution, very often personal testimony is taken as revelation, and we find it hard in any case to look lovingly

21. UNITY, DISUNITY, DIVERSITY

and without rancor at a friend and say, "This time, I think you may be wrong."

Moreover, there is a tension that is intrinsic to our understanding of divine–human relations between our love of unity as the true will of God and our imperative to speak Truth as we perceive it, even if others cannot agree.

The challenge (and sometimes the discouragement, too) lies in the acceptance that there is no foolproof way to be right, to know in the moment whether a message that is before us, or a messenger, is bringing us news sent by the Holy Spirit. Yet the experienced among us have tried from time to time to provide guidance about rules of thumb, the results of experiment and mistake. The ultimate aim of these advices is to help us recognize and prize a condition of health and strength, tenderness and courage, in which we can be alert to, and aware of, the Life of God in all. In the next section, I'd like to remind you of one such set of guideposts, from Isaac Penington, but I should point out that these advices lack one essential ingredient, which is how to continue to grow in our capacity for unity. I will return to this question in the final sections of this letter.

V. Moving towards unity, adjusting the balance

Isaac Penington was well acquainted with the tensions that arise in a body that is seeking guidance from the Spirit when every member is a potential receiver and transmitter of guidance but none is infallibly accurate. He knew that he himself had not always gotten this right:

> Now it is also in my heart . . . to mention a few things which I have found helpful to me towards the preserving of me in unity with the body. Perhaps it may please the Lord to refresh some others by the mention of them, and to make them useful and helpful to them also.[15]

One of the reasons that Penington's writings are so valuable is that he is constantly aware of the inward face of our outward actions and words. Furthermore, he clearly sees that unity is not a destination or a product but a condition in which we dwell and that we can help (not single-handedly!) to preserve. His four main points are both places to look for symptoms of disunity and ways to counteract that process.

> The first is, the pure fear of the Lord. This poiseth and guardeth the mind, keeping down fleshly confidence and conceitedness.[16]

If you examine yourself and find that you are placing too much confidence in your skills, standing, personality, or gifts, then you are not standing in the "pure fear of the Lord," that awareness of God's intimate and transcendent presence in whose life we need to ground all spiritual discernment. Returning to an awareness of this is a way to place ourselves (our fears and our powers) in perspective. Most important, this "fear" includes an alertness to God's presence at work in each of us, including those with whom our unity is threatened.

Penington's other "preserving points" need little comment but much consideration:

> The second is, humility of heart. This is very precious, and of a preserving nature. Yea, in this state the Lord helpeth and teacheth; and the soul also (in this state) is fit to receive the help and teachings of the Lord....

> A third great help, which in the tender mercy of the Lord I have had experience of, is sobriety of judgment. Not to value or set up mine own judgment, or that which I account the judgment of life in me, above the judgment of others, or that which is indeed life in others. For the Lord hath appeared in others, as well as to me; yea, there are others who are in the growth of his truth, and in the purity and dominion of his life, far beyond me. Now for me to set up, or hold forth, a sense or judgment of

21. UNITY, DISUNITY, DIVERSITY

anything in opposition to them, this is out of the sobriety which is of the truth. Therefore, in such cases, I am to retire, and fear before the Lord, and wait upon him for a clear discerning and sense of his truth, in the unity and demonstration of his Spirit with others, who are of him, and see him.

The last thing which I have now to mention is, tenderness, meekness, coolness, and stillness of spirit. I wrap up these together, because they are much of a nature, and go much together. These are of a uniting, preserving nature. He that differs and divides from the body cannot be thus; and he that is thus cannot rend or divide.[17]

Now, this kind of reflective inner work is hard to do in isolation; we often need help from our Friends. Even when we are in tension with our community, the community can offer resources for the work. In this connection, some people would suggest that Quakers need to reach to the concept of gospel order to help support unity and the dispositions that allow us to live in a unifying way. This is surely a valuable notion to include here, though it is not enough.

VI. Gospel order and homeostasis in the body of Christ—A part of the way forward

Thanks to Lewis Benson, and more recently to Lloyd Lee Wilson and Sondra Cronk,[18] Friends have become more widely aware of the notion of gospel order as promulgated by Fox. A most expansive approach to gospel order would define it as the social result of the free operation of the Spirit to create a coherent community practice under its guidance; some, as Bill Taber did, would connect it with what they see as the divine impulse ordering the functioning of all creation on every scale.

Fox speaks eloquently of how the power of God can be felt bringing order and unity; indeed, you might say that, in discerning spirits, a spirit that scatters is to be distrusted, however much it might be welcomed by some as a truthful spirit. After all, God is not *either* truthful *or* orderly; God is all things at once, and when we encounter God stuff, we encounter what feels like truth, or mercy, or justice, or conviction of sin, or comfort, or challenge—these are all different ways we experience the One.

> Fox writes:
> Because the Seed is one which is Christ and he is the Master . . . all brethren, who are in the Spirit, are one. You have all one Eye, which is the Light; one fire, which consumes all which the Light discovers to be evil; and one Spirit, that baptizes all into the one body, where there is no confusion, but pureness and oneness.[19]

Even though we are led by an infallible spirit, stability and persistence in faithfulness are a constantly maintained condition—homeostasis in the body of Christ. Fox continues: "Therefore, all Friends mind the oneness and that which keeps you in the oneness and unity."[20] Fox, like any perceptive member of a people, recognizes that it is possible to wander (jump, run) out of the Light and thus out of the oneness; we can be led into oneness by minding the Seed, but we can separate again. Thus, even for those who tend to speak of gospel order as an emergent, Spirit-guided structure, there is an assumption that, at least from the human point of view, the work of gospel order includes an inherent element of reconciliation and repair and thus connects with what might be called the "narrowest" interpretation of the term, that based on Matthew 18, in which Jesus recommends how to settle disagreements in the community.

Friends who stress the cosmic implications of gospel order see truly the continuity between the order that arises when a person or a people are most open and obedient to the Holy Spirit and the work of that same Spirit that enables us to see the need for reconciliation and strengthens us to seek

21. UNITY, DISUNITY, DIVERSITY

it. Although the group can be led into right action and the Spirit can help us discover community structure consistent with its guidance, the individuals are the living stones of the unity, the factors in the structure. *We must each dwell in faithfulness if we hope to be led faithfully as a people.*

In this mind, we are led away from any temptation to see gospel order solely in terms of a machinery (process) to be deployed to solve a problem or to intervene once something has gone wrong. While such processes and procedures can be powerful tools in the hand of a community or an individual in doubt or difficulty, they are not enough. Like any tool, they must be deployed at the appropriate time and applied effectively to the appropriate problems. To switch metaphors, medication is most helpful if you have a good diagnosis and you have chosen the correct intervention and dosage.

A persistent challenge for us in our Quaker struggles is that our diagnoses and prescriptions often do not rest on good analysis of our condition. We can be distracted by the confusion of personality with revelation; we can forget that a crisis in a community has a gestation period and that a disrupting or alarming event very often gains power from preexisting, often unnoticed, conditions—individuals' criticisms or doubts, crises of confidence or faith, unresolved grudges, hasty judgments, or a technical mindset that can perhaps close the lips of a wound but not wait and work for healing.

All our admonitions to be cool, tolerant, patient, to listen well, to use "I" statements, and so on, do not preserve and restore unity but only its appearance. If we do not allow ourselves to (require ourselves to, long for the power to, cry out for help to) learn from the Spirit lessons about our condition, about our current ability to enact unity, and about the things that hinder that acting, then our intellectual and emotional labor, our discussions and reports, will not move us forward.

VII. How are love and unity maintained?

With the lessons from history, the guidance of the wise in our tradition, and our own psychological and spiritual experience, we can see, perhaps, that unity is not an achievement but a way, the way of watchful living. We can see, too, what this dynamic state will look and feel like. Yet, knowing the goal is not the same as reaching it. It is also not the same as being able to get there. Becoming more able, more capable in the life of the Spirit, is the center of our work right now.

Yet, if we are not very teachable, very humble, and very determined, we will not be equipped to draw from the power and guidance of the Spirit, and we will fall back on our own strength, our own wisdom, and our own methods. We will bring into being an order that is not unrelated to the life of the gospel, the sweet and ardent Spirit, but is not rooted there. Our former experiences, revelations, and faithfulnesses are not useless, but the now, the present moment and condition, must be brought to the Spirit, and our hands, minds, and hearts must be open to three questions if we hope to play a part in the building up or healing of the life in the community.

1. Have I sought the Life of God in myself and in the others with whom I am engaged?

Here is a thing to wait for—to become still enough, cool enough, and expectant enough that we can feel our way to the place where the divine life is flowing in the measure we have received to this point. When a scientist prepares to take measurements, even so simple a thing as measuring temperature, they need to make sure that the instrument is calibrated so that the readings can be relied upon and compared with readings taken before, perhaps by someone

21. UNITY, DISUNITY, DIVERSITY

else, and also with readings taken in days or years to come, perhaps by yet a different investigator.

In an analogous fashion, we need to make sure that we do what it takes to be present with the Spirit that is not us, whose life is available to all, and in which we can have unity—first with ourselves and then with others. It may take a few minutes, it may take hours of patient waiting, but it is indispensable. If we cannot move past the place of anger and argument, look past grievances and fears, then we have not yet involved God in the process, however much we wish to. In this case, to pray for guidance includes this very active search for the place of truthful encounter with the Listener to prayer. We cannot answer that of God in the other if we have not first taken the time to recalibrate with that of God in ourselves—for it is the one Life that is the substance of unity.

2. Where is the Seed oppressed in myself and in others?

In the process of traveling to a renewed sense of the Presence, it is common enough to encounter resistance. You think you've gotten centered, and a persistent voice utters fears, objections, or desires; formulates speeches, defenses or complaints or questions; replays painful or puzzling scenes. You think you've settled down, but you discover your shoulders are still tensed, your legs wound tight, your jaw knotted.

The meditation masters will tell you not to struggle with these things, to look past them, to patiently unclench, to set the persistent mind aside, and to seek quiet again. Don't be distracted! But in the process of unity, of unifying, these nagging problems are evidence, evidence of places or processes in which the Seed is obscured, burdened, cramped, or stifled. Here, with the guidance and empowerment of the Spirit, is where the work of liberation must next take place.

3. What lessons should we learn from the Spirit of Christ?

In a time when our society is less and less able to name and point to outward unifiers, leaving us reliant on ourselves or (hopefully) the Spirit, it is essential to ask, Which Spirit is guiding me? How can I know its voice or activity?

The traditional Quaker response to this was to point out that the Light we follow, the Spirit whose guidance we seek, is in some sense in unity with Christ. After all, the peace testimony, which hangs on so many of our meeting walls, says, in part, "The Spirit of Christ by which we are led is not changeable, so as once to command us from a thing as evil and then to move us unto it."[21] Modern Friends react to this identification in a variety of ways, positive, negative, certain, uncertain. Yet I have found that to engage with the Spirit, as the Spirit of Christ, is to engage with a living teacher whose character is known—in part. In this engagement, for all its complexity, we are offered guidance and insight as we seek to free the Seed from the places of its oppression in ourselves and others, and we are given guidance as well to help us reflect upon our process.

We can thus ask ourselves if we are showing the outcome of authentic faithfulness in this Spirit, remembering that *the fruit of the spirit is love, joy, peace, longsuffering, gentleness, goodness, faith, meekness, temperance* (Galatians 5:22–23). Are we peacemakers, are we growing in mercy, are we growing in meekness, is our hunger and thirst for righteousness both aroused and satisfied? But these questions are still about *effects*, evidence of the Life, and so are only part of the diagnosis and teaching of the Spirit. How do we reach beyond these good things to understand what is hindering us from a fuller experience of the Light and Life? This is not a cognitive process, not a psychological process, not a verbal process. It lies in confrontation with the living Teacher.

In asking ourselves what in our condition prevents us from seeing and speaking for that of God, both in ourselves and the other, do we allow ourselves to be interrogated by

21. UNITY, DISUNITY, DIVERSITY

Christ himself, by whose spirit we claim to be guided? In our present dilemmas, the questions that come to mind as most important are these:

- Have you, have we, shared in Christ's doubt?

Return to the Gethsemane story and reflect on Jesus' agony of self-questioning there, accented by the sleepy inattention of his closest followers. Unlike them, he was aware that things might not work out; he questioned his own capacity when they did not. Just a few hours before, he and his friends had celebrated the Passover—a multiple miracle as God's sentence of death had passed over the Jews, the pharaoh's heart had been softened, and the people walked free, freed to move from outward oppression to a journey of struggle with self and God. Here was Jesus, once again wondering about the clarity of the Lord's intent for him, about his own faithfulness, and about the darkness of the nearest future. At his baptism, he was accompanied by a dove and a voice; after his temptations, he was ministered to in the wilderness. In Gethsemane, we hear no voice, see no assurance. With no such heavenly sign, Jesus accepts his cup, and wakening his earthly companions, is greeted by the arresting soldiers. We see no sign of divine support, as earthly reassurance and company desert him; and on the cross, at a time when he can forgive his executioners, care for his mother, feel his body's pain, he expresses the opposite of certainty: *"My God, my God, why hast thou forsaken me?"* (Mark 15:34).

- Have you, have we, learned with Christ about humility and teachableness?

Revisit the story told in Mark, of Jesus' encounter with the Syro-phoenician woman (Mark 7:24–30). Jesus has come to the hills near Tyre and Sidon for retreat. A woman not of the Jews nevertheless gets to him and asks the healer to free her daughter of a demon. Jesus refuses in terms that strike the reader as xenophobic bitterness: "It's not good to take the children's food and throw it to dogs." The woman turns the cheek, does not address the harshness of the remark, but instead says, "Even the dogs can eat the crumbs under the children's table." Jesus says, "Because of this word of yours, the demon has already left your daughter." It seems to me that the woman's strength and prophetic meekness touched the Witness in Jesus. He described himself as *meek and lowly in heart* (Matthew 11:29 KJV), and here is an example of it.

• Have you, have we, sought where forgiveness is required of us? Have we considered the forms that forgiveness can take?

At the end of the gospel accounts, after one failure after another, including abandonment and denial, Peter is still hanging in with Jesus. Jesus, triumphantly present after death, is nevertheless withdrawing his visible guidance — soon, even his spiritualized body will depart from view. In the last moment of quiet conversation, Jesus leads Peter through an exchange that seems clearly to show that Jesus is fully aware of Peter's panicked denials. The threefold probing of Peter's love is not followed by a rebuke, such as, "Now look, we both know you're not the most dependable guy in the clutch, but I'm going to try one more time here . . ." Instead, Jesus, who knew what was in the human heart, bids Peter to move beyond words of love to the work of love and to do that without reservation.

• Have you, have we, learned how joy comes, even while living in the cross?

Even while preparing for his final trials, Jesus speaks of joy and of the peace that the world cannot give. *We have not heard the good news of life in the Spirit, nor begun in some measure to live it, if we cannot claim this reward.*

21. UNITY, DISUNITY, DIVERSITY

The joy is not a negation of the pain, nor of the need for liberation; it is not the satisfaction of a job well done, nor of conformity with, harmony with, our friends and peers, for these are conditional and dependent upon many factors that can fluctuate like the weather. The peace we seek, and that Jesus offers, is something that can persist even through Gethsemane and through the struggle of emancipation from a dearly held shield against the Light.

Friends, if this peace is shattered, then we know that our unity with the Spirit is disturbed. There is no more important task than to seek again in every dusty corner, under every stone and clod, for this precious thing—the pearl of great price, the poor woman's little coin.

In Christian love, your friend,

Brian Drayton

Bibliography

Allen, Richard C., and Moore, Rosemary. *The Quakers 1656–1723*. University Park: Pennsylvania State University Press, 2018.

The Apostolic Fathers, Vol. 1. Translated by Kirsopp Lake. Loeb Classical Library #24. Cambridge, MA: Harvard University Press, 1912.

Benson, Lewis. "The People of God and Gospel Order." In *The Church in Quaker Thought and Practice*, edited by Charles F. Thomas, 16–29. Philadelphia: Friends World Committee for Consultation, 1979.

Bownas, Samuel. *A Description of the Qualifications Necessary to a Gospel Minister*. Wallingford, PA: Pendle Hill Publications, 1989.

Braithwaite, W. C. *The Beginnings of Quakerism*. 2nd edition. Cambridge: Cambridge University Press, 1955.

Britain Yearly Meeting. *Quaker Faith and Practice: The Book of Christian Discipline of the Yearly Meeting of the Religious Society of Friends (Quakers) in Britain*. Warwick, UK: The Yearly Meeting of the Religious Society of Friends (Quakers) in Britain, 1995.

Britten, William. *Silent meeting, a wonder to the world, yet practiced by the Apostles, and owned by the people of God, scornfully called Quakers*. London: printed for Robert Wilson, 1660.

Cronk, Sandra L. *Gospel Order: A Quaker Understanding of Faithful Church Community*. Pendle Hill Pamphlet #297. Wallingford, PA: Pendle Hill Publications, 1991.

Drayton, Brian. *Climate change a spiritual challenge and Becoming again a witnessing body: Two Letters to New England Friends*. Quaker Issues BHFH-1013. Boston: Beacon Hill Friends House, 2012.

———. "It doesn't have to be this way: Proclaiming gospel values, with a note on 'original sin.'" *Amor Vincat* (blog). March 28, 2021. https://amorvincat.wordpress.com/2021/03/28/it-doesnt-have-to-be-this-way-proclaiming-gospel-values-with-a-note-on-original-sin/.

———. "Nurturing the Seed of Christ: An Epistle." *Friends Bulletin* (April 2008): 15–16.

———. "'That of God in every one': Can we not say a little more?" *Amor Vincat* (blog). August 8, 2020. https://wordpress.com/post/amorvincat.wordpress.com/1502.

———. "To Friends, not to reason and judge too much about gifts, but to listen to the Witness, and not to fear." *Amor Vincat* (blog). https://amorvincat.wordpress.com/2019/11/15/to-friends-not-to-reason-and-judge-too-much-about-gifts-but-to-listen-to-the-witness-and-not-to-fear/.

———. *Unity, disunity, diversity or Some mysteries of the Holy Spirit's life at work in its body's members: A Letter to New England Friends.* Boston: Beacon Hill Friends House, 2007.

Erasmus, Desiderius. *Novum Testamentum ab Erasmo recognitum III.* Edited by A. J. Brown. Opera Omnia 6.3. Amsterdam: Elsevier, 2003.

Erasmus, Desiderius. *Paraphrasis in epistolam Pauli ad Romanos.* Edited by Jean Leclercq. Opera Omnia Des. Erasmis Roterodami Tomus VII. Leiden, 1705.

Fox, George. *The Journal of George Fox.* Edited by John L. Nickalls. Cambridge: Cambridge University Press, 1952.

Gwyn, Douglas. *Seekers Found: Atonement in Early Quaker Experience.* Wallingford, PA: Pendle Hill Publications, 2001.

Jones, T. Canby. *The Power of the Lord Is Over All: The Pastoral Letters of George Fox.* Richmond, IN: Friends United Press, 1989.

Moore, Rosemary. *The Light in Their Consciences: The Early Quakers in Britain, 1646–1666.* University Park: Pennsylvania State University Press, 2000.

Nayler, James. *The Works of James Nayler.* Vols. 1–4. Glenside, PA: Quaker Heritage Press, 2003–2009.

Neelon, David. *James Nayler: Revolutionary to Prophet.* Becket, MA: Leadings Press, 2009.

Norlind, Emilia Fogelklou. *The Atonement of George Fox.* Pendle Hill Pamphlet #166. Wallingford, PA: Pendle Hill Publications, 1969.

Penington, Isaac. *The Works of Isaac Penington, a Minister of the Gospel in the Society of Friends.* Vols. 1–4. Glenside, PA: Quaker Heritage Press, 1995–1997.

Penn, William. *The Rise and Progress of the People Called Quakers.* Reprint edition. Richmond, IN: Friends United Press, 1980.

Rowntree, Joshua, ed. *John Wilhelm Rowntree: Essays and Addresses.* London: Headley Brothers, 1905.

Scott, Job. *The works of that eminent minister of the Gospel, Job Scott, late of Providence, Rhode Island.* 2 vols. Philadelphia: John Comly, 1831.

Smith, Edward. *William Dewsbury, c1621–1688: One of the First Valiant Sixty Quakers* [1836]. York, UK: Sessions of York, 1997. https://www.hallvworthington.com/Dewsbury/Bio-1.html.

Taber, William P., Jr. "The Unity Underlying Quaker Diversity." In *Realignment: Nine Views among Friends*, 1–10. Pendle Hill Monday Evening Lecture Series. Wallingford, PA: Pendle Hill Publications, 1991.

Wilson, Lloyd Lee. *Essays on the Quaker Vision of Gospel Order.* Wallingford, PA: Pendle Hill Publications, 1993.

Woolman, John. *The Journal and Major Essays of John Woolman.* Edited by Phillips P. Moulton. New York: Oxford University Press, 1971.

NOTES

3. Awesome: Psalm 111 and true worship (pp. 9–13)

[1] Isaac Penington, *The Works of Isaac Penington, a Minister of the Gospel in the Society of Friends* (Glenside, PA: Quaker Heritage Press, 1995), 1:36.

[2] James Nayler, "A Discovery," in *The Works of James Nayler* (Glenside, PA: Quaker Heritage Press, 2003), 1:51.

[3] James Nayler, *Love to the Lost*, in *The Works of James Nayler* (Glenside, PA: Quaker Heritage Press, 2007), 3:63.

[4] Early Friends sometimes spoke of the Lamb's War (echoing John 1:29, Revelation 5, and elsewhere) against the Man of Sin (2 Thessalonians 2:3). Nayler wrote a powerful tract by that title in 1657 (*Works* 4:1–20). The life engaged in the Lamb's War is made tender and is opened to see and oppose injustice and violence outwardly as well as inwardly by the work of Lamb, who is Christ the Light. Your soul is a meeting place of forces tending both to your good and ill. Some of the evils can be seen as external—sources of fear, oppression, or distraction. Others are apparently inward—anger, self-indulgence, and so on. Inward and outward forces activate or counteract each other. Because it is this kind of meeting place, the human soul is an appropriate battlefield upon which to begin the war against "outward" evils in the world. More than this—if the battle remains unfought in any soul, then in our unredeemed regions, seeds of sin and death lie as in an incubator, from which they can spread abroad anew. Hence, the Lamb's War requires witness against oppression and injustice of all kinds.

4. As we reflect on our meetings' spiritual condition: A letter to my Friends (pp. 14–19)

[1] George Fox, Epistle 264, in T. Canby Jones, *The Power of the Lord is Over All: The Pastoral Letters of George Fox* (Richmond, IN: Friends United Press, 1989). pp. 254–55.

5. Climate change a spiritual challenge (pp. 20–27)

[1] Brian Drayton, *Climate Change a spiritual challenge and Becoming again a witnessing body: Two letters to New England Friends*, Quaker Issues BHFH-1013 (Boston: Beacon Hill Friends House, 2012).

[2] George Fox, *The Journal of George Fox*, ed. John L. Nickalls (Cambridge: Cambridge University Press, 1952), 11.

[3] Fox, *Journal of George Fox*, 98.

[4] William Penn, *The Rise and Progress of the People Called Quakers*, reprint ed. (Richmond, IN: Friends United Press, 1980), 38.

6. Becoming again a witnessing body (pp. 28–32)

[1] Drayton *Climate Change*.

7. To ministers and elders gathering in West Brattleboro (pp. 33–34)

[1] Samuel Bownas, *A Description of the Qualifications Necessary to a Gospel Minister* (Wallingford, PA: Pendle Hill Publications, 1989).

8. To Friends, not to reason and judge too much about gifts (pp. 35–38)

[1] Brian Drayton, "To Friends, not to reason and judge too much about gifts, but to listen to the Witness, and not to fear," *Amor Vincat* (blog), Nov. 15, 2019.

9. To Fresh Pond Meeting (pp. 39–42)

[1] Isaac Penington, "Some directions to the panting soul" [1661], in *The Works of Isaac Penington, a Minister of the Gospel in the Society of Friends* (Glenside, PA: Quaker Heritage Press, 1994), 2:202–3.

11. The fear of the Lord is our treasure (pp. 45–47)

[1] Fox, *Journal of George Fox*, 71.

[2] The demi-god Hercules, who in madness had killed his family, was set to serve Eurystheus, king of Mycenae, for twelve years as penance. He was commanded to perform several apparently impossible feats. One was to kill a multiheaded serpent monster, the Hydra, which grew back two heads for each one hewn off. Later, seeking the Garden

of the Hesperides, he was challenged to battle by the giant Antaeus, whose strength grew whenever he was in contact with the earth.

12. Nurturing the Seed (pp. 48–51)

[1] Brian Drayton, "Nurturing the Seed of Christ: An Epistle," *Friends Bulletin* (April 2008): 15–16.

[2] Penn, *Rise and Progress*, 83.

[3] John Woolman, "A Plea for the Poor," in *The Journal and Major Essays of John Woolman*, ed. Phillips P. Moulton (New York: Oxford University Press, 1971), 241. The full quotation is: "Our gracious Creator cares and provides for all his creatures. His tender mercies are over all his works; and so far as his love influences our minds, so far we become interested in his workmanship and feel a desire to take hold of every opportunity to lessen the distresses of the afflicted and increase the happiness of the creation. Here we have a prospect of one common interest from which our own is inseparable, that to turn all the treasures we possess into the channel of universal love becomes the business of our lives."

13. Not to be discouraged by the great challenges before us (pp. 52–54)

[1] Fox, *Journal of George Fox*, 103.

[2] Rowntree, "Testimony of Pickering and Hull Monthly Meeting, respecting John Wilhelm Rowntree, a minister, deceased," in *John Wilhelm Rowntree: Essays and Addresses*, ed. Joshua Rowntree (London: Headley Brothers, 1905), xlvii.

[3] Scott, *Journal*, in *The works of that eminent minister of the Gospel, Job Scott, late of Providence, Rhode Island* (Philadelphia: John Comly, 1831, 1:13. Job Scott (1751–1793) was a widely respected minster from New England. He traveled widely in the ministry, and he died of smallpox while visiting Ireland. His journal and other writings, published posthumously, present a Quakerism closely related to that preached by early Friends, and his theology is creative and sometimes daring.

14. Friends, welcome prophets among us in these dark times! (pp. 55–57)

[1] The *Didache* is a little document that might be seen as a very early book of discipline. It is generally thought to date from the first century CE. Though there are references to it in early Christian literature, the text was lost until 1873. "Didache," in *The Apostolic Fathers, Vol. 1*, trans. Kirsopp Lake, Loeb Classical Library #24 (Cambridge, MA: Harvard University Press, 1912), 305–33.

15. It doesn't have to be this way (pp. 58–62)

[1] The phrase is borrowed from the title of a book by G. H. C. MacGregor, *The New Testament Basis of Pacifism and the Relevance of an Impossible Ideal* (1954).

[2] Margaret Fell, "Testimony to the Life of George Fox." This is most easily found in Britain Yearly Meeting's *Quaker Book of Faith and Practice: The Book of Christian Discipline of the Yearly Meeting of the Religious Society of Friends (Quakers) in Britain* (Warwick, UK: The Yearly Meeting of the Religious Society of Friends (Quakers) in Britain, 1995), §19.07.

[3] Penington, "Some queries concerning the order and government of the Church of Christ," in *Works of Isaac Penington*, 2:371–72.

[4] Desiderius Erasmus, *Novum Testamentum ab Erasmo recognitum III*, ed. A. J. Brown, *Opera Omnia* 6.3 (Amsterdam: Elsevier, 2003).

[5] William Wordsworth, "Ode on Intimations of Immortality" (1807).

17. To Friendship Meeting (pp. 65–67)

[1] Woolman, *Journal and Major Essays of John Woolman*, 31.

19. Building our house in the storm (pp. 70–72)

[1] Woolman, *Journal and Major Essays of John Woolman*, 156.

20. "That of God in every one" (pp. 73–76)

[1] Woolman, *A plea for the poor* [1763–64], in *Journal and Major Essays of John Woolman*, 250.

[2] Fox, *Journal of George Fox*, 27–28.

[3] This quotation is from the 1660 "A declaration from the harmless and innocent people of God called Quakers," often called the peace testimony, in Fox, *Journal of George Fox*, 399.

NOTES

21. Unity, disunity, diversity (pp. 77–102)

[1] Drayton, *Unity, disunity, diversity or Some mysteries of the Holy Spirit's life at work in its body's members: A Letter to New England Friends* (Boston: Beacon Hill Friends House, 2007).

[2] Friends United Meeting (FUM), the largest umbrella association of Friends in North America (not to mention its even larger membership in Africa and Latin America), includes members across the theological spectrum from very liberal to very evangelical. Some of its meetings are "united," that is, they experienced some or all of the Quaker schisms of the nineteenth century but reunited, starting with New England in 1945. As a result, these united meetings belong both to the avowedly Christian FUM, and to the liberal Friends General Conference. The theological differences embodied in these united meetings have caused tensions within FUM over the years. In the early 1990s, some FUM Friends suggested that the member yearly meetings of FUM "realign," with the evangelical groups joining in some fashion with the Evangelical Friends International and the liberal groups joining in some fashion with Friends General Conference. This movement, which caused much controversy and reflection, never succeeded in the envisioned reshaping of Quaker organization.

[3] William P. Taber, Jr., "The Unity Underlying Quaker Diversity," in *Realignment: Nine Views among Friends*, Pendle Hill Monday Evening Lecture Series (Wallingford, PA: Pendle Hill Publications, 1991), 3.

[4] Francis Howgill, as quoted in Britain Yearly Meeting, *Quaker Faith and Practice*, chap. 19, sec. 8.

[5] Fox, *Journal of George Fox*, 621.

[6] In the fall of 1656, Nayler was led in a sorry re-enactment of Jesus' entry into Jerusalem through the gates of Bristol, with a few followers shouting "Holy, Holy, Holy, Lord God of Hosts." Nayler was arrested and was eventually tried and convicted as a blasphemer by Parliament itself. Nayler was publicly humiliated and severely tortured, and he was incarcerated for the rest of the decade. After his reconciliation with Friends, he resumed writing, and after his release in 1660 he took up public ministry again. He died after being assaulted on the road home to Yorkshire in 1660. For more on the re-enactment, see Douglas Gwyn, *Seekers Found: Atonement in Early Quaker Experience* (Wallingford, PA: Pendle Hill Publications,

2001); David Neelon, *James Nayler: Revolutionary to Prophet* (Becket, MA: Leadings Press, 2009).

⁷ James Nayler, *The Works of James Nayler* (Glenside, PA: Quaker Heritage Press, 209), 4:266–67.

⁸ William Dewsbury, as quoted in Edward Smith, *William Dewsbury, c1621–1688: One of the First Valiant Sixty Quakers* [1836] (York, UK: Sessions of York, 1997), https://www.hallvworthington.com/Dewsbury/Bio-1.html, 108.

⁹ William Dewsbury, as quoted in Smith, *William Dewsbury*, 148.

¹⁰ By 1670, many of the "Valiant 60" had already died during the fierce persecutions of the previous decade, including James Nayler, William Caton, John Camm, Francis Howgill, Richard Hubberthorne, Edward Burrough, Samuel Fisher, George Fox "the younger," and Richard Farnsworth. Other prominent leaders, such as William Dewsbury, Isaac Penington, Robert Barclay, and George Fox himself, spent months or years in prison during the 1670s and 1680s.

¹¹ This letter is an important forerunner of later books of discipline. A gathering of leading ministers spent time considering the spiritual condition of the meetings they had visited (and often had helped establish) and were led to draft some guidelines for maintaining (or reestablishing) healthy meetings. A good description and outline may be found in W. C. Braithwaite, *The Beginnings of Quakerism*, 2nd ed. (Cambridge: Cambridge University Press, 1955), 310–313; see also Rosemary Moore, *The Light in Their Consciences: The Early Quakers in Britain, 1646–1666* (University Park: Pennsylvania State University Press, 2000), 137–38. William Dewsbury and Richard Farnworth were key contributors. One paragraph from the letter is quoted widely in books of faith and practice: "Dearly beloved Friends, these things we do not lay upon you as a rule to walk by, but that all with the measure of light which is pure and holy may be guided, and so in the light walking and abiding, these may be fulfilled in the Spirit—not from the letter, for the letter killeth, but the Spirit giveth life."

¹² A good treatment of the controversy can be found Braithwaite, *The Beginnings of Quakerism*, 290–323; Richard C. Allen and Rosemary Moore, *The Quakers 1656–1723* (University Park: Pennsylvania State University Press, 2018), 65–75.

¹³ Emerson's remark can be found in his 1841 essay "Self-Reliance." For an account of how Fox "replaced himself," see Emilia Fogelklou

NOTES

Norlind, *The Atonement of George Fox*, Pendle Hill Pamphlet #166 (Wallingford, PA: Pendle Hill Publications, 1969).

[14] William Dewsbury, April 1678, to unknown recipient, as quoted in Braithwaite, *The Beginnings of Quakerism*, 318.

[15] Penington, "Some queries concerning the order and government of the Church of Christ," in *Works of Isaac Penington*, 2:371.

[16] Penington, "Some queries concerning the order and government of the Church of Christ," in *Works of Isaac Penington*, 2:371–72.

[17] Penington, "Some queries concerning the order and government of the Church of Christ," in *Works of Isaac Penington*, 2:371-72.

[18] The concept of gospel order as understood by Friends is developed in Lewis Benson, "The People of God and Gospel Order," in *The Church in Quaker Thought and Practice*, ed. Charles F. Thomas (Philadelphia: Friends World Committee for Consultation, 1979), 16–29; Sandra L. Cronk, *Gospel Order: A Quaker Understanding of Faithful Church Community*, Pendle Hill Pamphlet #297 (Wallingford, PA: Pendle Hill Publications, 1991); and Lloyd Lee Wilson, *Essays on the Quaker Vision of Gospel Order* (Wallingford, PA: Pendle Hill Publications, 1993).

[19] Fox, Epistle 46, in Jones, *The Power of the Lord*, 39.

[20] Fox, Epistle 46, in Jones, *The Power of the Lord*, 39.

[21] "A Declaration from the harmless and innocent people of God called Quakers" [1660], in Fox, *Journal of George Fox*, 399.

Also available from Inner Light Books

Movings of Divine Love: The Love of God in the Letters of John Woolman
by Drew Lawson
    ISBN 978-1-7346300-3-9 (hardcover)
    ISBN 978-1-7346300-4-6 (paperback)
    ISBN 978-1-7346300-5-3 (eBook)

A Call to Friends: Faithful Living in Desperate Times
By Marty Grundy
    ISBN 978–1-7346300–6–0 (hardcover)
    ISBN 978–1-7346300–7-7 (paperback)
    ISBN 978–1-7346300–8-4 (eBook)

Surrendering into Silence: Quaker Prayer Cycles
By David Johnson
    ISBN 978–1-7346300–0-8 (hardcover)
    ISBN 978–1-7346300–1-5 (paperback)
    ISBN 978–1-7346300–2-2 (eBook)

A Guide to Faithfulness Groups
By Marcelle Martin
    ISBN 978-1-7328239-4-5 (hardcover)
    ISBN 978-1-7328239-5-2 (paperback)
    ISBN 978-1-7328239-6-9 (eBook)

A Word from the Lost: Remarks on James Nayler's Love to the Lost
By David Lewis
    ISBN 978-1-7328239-7-6 (hardcover)
    ISBN 978-1-7328239-8-3 (paperback)
    ISBN 978-1-7328239-9-0 (eBook)

William Penn's 'Holy Experiment'
by James Proud
    ISBN 978-0-9998332-9-2 (hardcover)
    ISBN 978-1-7328239-3-8 (paperback)

In the Stillness: Poems, prayers, reflections
by Elizabeth Mills
    ISBN 978-1-7328239-0-7 (hardcover)
    ISBN 978-1-7328239-1-4 (paperback)
    ISBN 978-1-7328239-2-1 (eBook)

Walk Humbly, Serve Boldly: Modern Quakers as Everyday Prophets
by Margery Post Abbott
    ISBN 978-0-9998332-6-1 (hardcover)
    ISBN 978-0-9998332-7-8 (paperback)
    ISBN 978-0-9998332-8-5 (eBook)

Primitive Quakerism Revived
by Paul Buckley
> ISBN 978-0-9998332-2-3 (hardcover)
> ISBN 978-0-9998332-3-0 (paperback)
> ISBN 978-0-9998332-5-4 (eBook)

Primitive Christianity Revived
by William Penn
Translated into Modern English by Paul Buckley
> ISBN 978-0-9998332-0-9 (hardcover)
> ISBN 978-0-9998332-1-6 (paperback)
> ISBN 978-0-9998332-4-7 (eBook)

Jesus, Christ and Servant of God
Meditations on the Gospel According to John
by David Johnson
> ISBN 978–0–9970604–6–1 (hardcover)
> ISBN 978–0–9970604–7–8 (paperback)
> ISBN 978–0–9970604–8–5 (eBook)

The Anti-War
by Douglas Gwyn
> ISBN 978-0-9970604-3-0 (hardcover)
> ISBN 978-0-9970604-4-7 (paperback)
> ISBN 978-0-9970604-5-4 (eBook)

Our Life Is Love, the Quaker Spiritual Journey
by Marcelle Martin
> ISBN 978-0-9970604-0-9 (hardcover)
> ISBN 978-0-9970604-1-6 (paperback)
> ISBN 978-0-9970604-2-3 (eBook)

A Quaker Prayer Life
by David Johnson
> ISBN 978-0-9834980-5-6 (hardcover)
> ISBN 978-0-9834980-6-3 (paperback)
> ISBN 978-0-9834980-7-0 (eBook)

The Essential Elias Hicks
by Paul Buckley
> ISBN 978-0-9834980-8-7 (hardcover)
> ISBN 978-0-9834980-9-4 (paperback)
> ISBN 978-0-9970604-9-2 (eBook)

The Journal of Elias Hicks
edited by Paul Buckley
> ISBN 978-0-9797110-4-6 (hardcover)
> ISBN 978-0-9797110-5-3 (paperback)

Dear Friend: The Letters and Essays of Elias Hicks
edited by Paul Buckley
        ISBN 978-0-9834980-0-1 (hardcover)
        ISBN 978-0-9834980-1-8 (paperback)

The Early Quakers and 'the Kingdom of God'
by Gerard Guiton
        ISBN 978-0-9834980-2-5 (hardcover)
        ISBN 978-0-9834980-3-2 (paperback)
        ISBN 978-0-9834980-4-9 (eBook)

John Woolman and the Affairs of Truth
edited by James Proud
        ISBN 978-0-9797110-6-0 (hardcover)
        ISBN 978-0-9797110-7-7 (paperback)

Cousin Ann's Stories for Children by Ann Preston
edited by Richard Beards
illustrated by Stevie French
        ISBN 978-0-9797110-8-4 (hardcover),
        ISBN 978-0-9797110-9-1 (paperback)

Counsel to the Christian-Traveller: also Meditations and Experiences
by William Shewen
        ISBN 978-0-9797110-0-8 (hardcover)
        ISBN 978-0-9797110-1-5 (paperback)

www.ingramcontent.com/pod-product-compliance
Lightning Source LLC
Chambersburg PA
CBHW020941090426
42736CB00010B/1220